Casting the First Stone

The Hypocrisy of
Religious Fundamentalism
and its Threat to Society

R. A. Gilbert

ELEMENT
Shaftesbury, Dorset ● Rockport, Massachusetts
Brisbane, Queensland

Published in Great Britain in 1993 by
Element Books Limited
Longmead, Shaftesbury, Dorset

Published in the USA in 1993 by
Element Inc.
42 Broadway, Rockport, MA 01966

Published in Australia in 1993 by
Element Books Limited for
Jacaranda Wiley Limited
33 Park Road, Milton, Brisbane 4064

Cover design by Max Fairbrother
Designed by Roger Lightfoot
Typeset by The Electronic Book Factory Ltd, Fife, Scotland
Printed and bound in Great Britain by
Dotesios Ltd, Trowbridge, Wiltshire

British Library Cataloguing in Publication
data available

Library of Congress Cataloging in Publication
data available

ISBN 1-85230-367-0

Contents

Preface

It would be easy to step back from this book and smugly to proclaim that its sole inspiration was a passionate commitment to Voltaire's dictum that 'I disapprove of what you say, but I will defend to the death your right to say it.' I like to believe that I am motivated by such a sentiment. But if I am honest I must admit that there is also the matter of self-interest: my working life is bound up with my personal fascination for unorthodox beliefs; I may not subscribe to them but I am economically dependent upon those who hold them and who put them into practice. Any check upon their freedom to do so is a check upon my own livelihood.

In an ultimate sense we are, of course, all dependent on one another, and it serves no one's best interests to oppress his fellows. The need for global co-operation to husband our food and energy resources is recognized by responsible governments and individuals alike, but an awareness of that need has not filtered through to those in thrall to the forces of unreason. Nor will it do so without a conscious and determined effort on the part of all who believe in political, economic and religious freedom, as we strive to overcome the resurgence of ethnic and religious rivalries and hatreds that have followed the collapse of the monolithic power blocs of the former Communist world.

The dreadful alternative is to turn inwards and to build isolated, mutually hostile societies propagating their own brands of mutually exclusive religious and philosophical 'truth'. The risk of such a scenario is all too real: the murderous hatreds bringing chaos and despair to the former Yugoslavia are witness to that. And as our energies are occupied with separating physically warring peoples – who would not be so busily killing each other if their former rulers had practised the tolerance and equality they so emptily preached – they are turned from the task of feeding millions who needlessly starve.

Compared with the magnitude of these tasks, the effort of encouraging tolerance and mutual respect among those who differ over religious beliefs within a stable democracy may seem of little account. But unless true tolerance is encouraged – and taught by example – we shall see the flowing of bitter sectarian strife as the seeds of intolerance and bigotry grow and our own society becomes ever more divided and divisive. That those seeds continue to grow throughout Britain, Europe, North America and all the supposedly democratic world is all too evident. Hostility to alternative beliefs is still a prominent feature of the Christian fundamentalist way of life wherever it is found. In America the religious right continues its political march – evidenced by the rhetoric of Pat Buchanan at this year's Republican Convention, while the war against the New Age continues unabated in Britain, with Dianne Core still promoting the monstrous myth of Satanic Child Abuse. And beneath such high profile examples is a growing mountain of hysterical claims and absurd comments on every aspect of alternative or non-orthodox religions.

Nor is the hostility all one-sided. The pernicious practices that constitute 'Political Correctness' have become endemic in American academic life, blighting careers and devaluing true scholarship, while in Britain the supporters of traditional religious beliefs and practices face the venom of unreasoning and self-serving opponents who seem to seek change simply for its own sake. All that this achieves is an equally hysterical backlash that drives rational and humane men and women from both university and church, impoverishing both education and institutional religious life.

It is admittedly difficult to withstand naked hatred (indeed, it was doctrinal chaos that drove me to leave the Church of England) but if we wish to see humanity maintain all that makes it deserve the name, we must stand up and fight against unreason and intolerance, whether it be religious or political. And we must do that with neither anger nor the cynicism of Gibbon – who wrote that the religions of Rome were 'all considered by the people as equally true; by the philosopher, as equally false; and by the magistrate, as equally useful. And thus tolerance produced not only mutual indulgence, but even religious concord.' Admirable though this outcome may be, we shall not overcome the irrational forces we face by acknowledging bigoted beliefs as true; we must face them with love, but love tempered by reason. Only by understanding their true nature can we identify the falsity of their reasoning and thus be able to display them to the world for what they are and so defeat them.

R. A. Gilbert
September 1992

Acknowledgements

Compiling this book alone would have been an impossible task, and I have been fortunate in receiving the willing help of many. Although limitations of space preclude my mentioning all of them, some deserve especial mention for their ungrudging efforts on my belief. To John Michael I am indebted for the initial stimulus that led to this book and for much of the source material concerning cults and de-programming; John Hamill and John Bull gave me significant information on current attacks upon Freemasonry, while Jeremy Tribe has been a continuing and reliable source for details of the many fundamentalist campaigns against occultism; Tony Ortzen of *Psychic News* provided many examples of attacks upon Spiritualists; the Revd Kevin Tingay gave me the benefit of his own experiences, as did Dr Hugh Ormsby-Lennon of Philadelphia, while Mrs Beryl Statham produced a continuous flow of extracts from the local and national Press; and Sarah Townsend generously gave me copies of every printed account of the campaign of persecution against her. And, perhaps most heartening of all, I received nothing but courteous assistance from the staff of the ECL Bookshop in Bristol, who provided me with almost all of the published attacks on alternative beliefs that I have quoted throughout this book.

Faith under Fire

In her everyday life there is nothing to link Sarah Townsend, a Lincoln shopkeeper, with Jill Simpson, a teacher in Bucks County, Pennsylvania. But there is a tie that binds them together: a dark current that flows with increasing strength beneath the tolerant, liberal surface of Western society, emerging with increasing frequency to damage and destroy the lives of the innocent. It has brought unwarranted suffering into the lives of these two women and it forms the subject of this book.

On 28 January 1992, following a year-long campaign of public protest and harassment against 'Bridge of Dreams', Sarah Townsend's psychic bookshop at Lincoln, a petrol bomb burned out much of the shop and virtually destroyed Mrs Townsend's business. Fourteen months earlier, in December 1989, Jill Simpson's home at Langhorne was meticulously torn apart by police seeking evidence for persistent allegations of child abuse. They found nothing, but although Mrs Simpson was pronounced innocent, her career in teaching was ruined. In each case what lay behind the accusations, the hostility and the suffering were ignorance, credulity and intolerance relating to the same broad field of human experience – the occult – and derived from the same source: Christian fundamentalism.

It would, of course, be quite wrong to claim that religious fundamentalism, whether Christian or of any other faith, necessarily leads to persecution and repression, but by its very exclusivity it contains the seeds of intolerance within itself and often finds fertile soil in those who embrace fundamentalism. Nor can it be justly claimed that religious fundamentalism poses, at present, a general threat to the civil liberties of the entire population of the Western world; but on many occasions in the past social pressures in small and self-contained communities have generated religious fanaticism that has led to physical persecution and even to death.

The most obvious example is the false accusation, persecution and unjust punishment during the sixteenth and seventeenth centuries of innocent men, women and children in many parts of Europe, and in New England, on charges of witchcraft. Despite many thousands of books written in a vain attempt to prove the reality of 'witchcraft' and the crimes of the accused, no shred of evidence has ever withstood the cold light of objective analysis. But the accusations *were* made, the 'witches' *were* found guilty, and they suffered because of the fear, envy and misplaced religious zeal of their peers.

Could such events happen again? Alas, they could. Political repression is all too real, even in Western democracies: it should not be forgotten that it is little more than forty years since the first hearings of Senator McCarthy's 'Un-American Activities Committee' whose baseless tarring with the brush of Communism blighted the careers of so many prominent Americans. We do, admittedly, have checks and balances in our political systems that are designed to prevent such persecution, but these are legal restraints imposed by the tolerant that can be all too easily removed by the intolerant should the strains of our seemingly ever more uncertain and fearful society bring them to political power.

Even should such an event come about, we might yet take comfort in the sure knowledge that the complex make-up of the populations of Western countries tends to prevent such extreme polarizations of race and faith as occur in the Middle East and Southern Asia. But while we do not witness inter-racial and inter-religious atrocities on the scale of those that occur between Arab and Jew in Israel, between Hindu and Sikh in India, or between Buddhist and Hindu in Sri Lanka, we see the fruits of religious hatred in the death sentence imposed on Salman Rushdie, and in the sectarian violence of Northern Ireland. That unhappy province is reaping the harvest of political grievances cast in a religious mould, but religious intolerance is not necessarily driven by its political twin. Indeed, in both Britain and America, religious commitment – and thus the bigotry that may arise from it – is largely independent of political affiliation.

It does not follow, however, that this lessens the risk of religious intolerance, nor ultimately of an intolerance that is officially sanctioned. The increasingly complex racial and religious structure of the populations of Britain, America and other industrialized Western nations might be expected to lead to a growth in mutual understanding by the followers of different faiths, but this would require positive and dedicated education towards that end, and such education is rarely provided at any level by either national or local government. Thus faced with the presence of what are perceived as alien cultures and creeds in a wider society increasingly beset by social tensions, and an unpredictable political and social future, there are many in all Western countries who seek intellectual and spiritual refuge in the certainties of simplistic and dogmatic versions of their traditional faiths; that is, in religious fundamentalism.

This shift in religious beliefs and behaviour towards fundamentalism is not confined to Christians: it can also be observed among Muslims and Jews, but as the majority of people in western Europe and North America are nominally Christian, it is Christian fundamentalism in particular that is considered in this book, although a parallel rise in intolerance within the Jewish community cannot be ignored. It must be stressed again, however, that fundamentalism does not necessarily lead to intolerance, and by no means all fundamentalists would be in favour of persecuting those of other faiths. But enough of them *are* intolerant, and *do* persecute those who do not conform to their canons of moral and religious rectitude, to constitute a real threat to religious freedom, and to justify an analysis of their beliefs, aims and actions. Before any attempt to determine why fundamentalists are intolerant, however, it is essential first to consider in general terms who they persecute and what that persecution can involve.

In Britain most followers of Islam, Hinduism, Buddhism and other oriental religions are non-European and are, at least nominally, protected from physical and verbal harassment by the Race Relations Act of 1972. The same protection is not afforded to the followers of non-Christian Western religions, nor to members of the many 'New Religious Movements', nor to those active in the New Age movement (nor, for that matter, to Christians – whatever their denomination may be). And it is for all of these, together with the practitioners of alternative medicine and those who maintain unorthodox 'alternative' lifestyles, that the real venom of the fundamentalists is reserved. They are not perceived simply as alternatives to Christianity; instead they are all seen as spiritual enemies inspired by Satan who are to be engaged in battle and fought to final defeat.

If these battles were merely fought as a war of words, in the form of sermons preached to the converted, and books published for the faithful, they would pass unnoticed and would have little or no effect upon the lives of those being attacked. But they are not so limited in scope. The media – newspapers, radio and television – are persuaded, by way of sensational stories about the prevalence of witchcraft and Satanism, to give time and space to the claims and arguments of fundamentalists; their views are broadcast to a wider public, and credence is given to the utterly unjust notion that the New Age and all that it stands for, all alternative religious beliefs, and all the New Religious Movements are anti-Christian.

As a consequence of such hostile propaganda, all manifestations of the New Age and other targets of fundamentalist wrath are subject to various forms of harassment, ranging in degree from pulpit denunciations, through protest demonstrations outside psychic fairs and shops, to false accusations of criminal activity, and to kidnapping and fire-bombing. Those so persecuted face damage to both their public and their private lives, and the loss of health, reputation, career and livelihood. Even, on occasion, the loss of life itself.

The petrol-bomb that wrecked Sarah Townsend's shop cannot be proven to have been the work of fundamentalists, but even if it was not, it certainly followed a cruel, year-long campaign mounted by two fundamentalist organizations: the Reachout Trust and the New Life Christian Fellowship. A press campaign attacking the 'Bridge of Dreams' from the time of its opening in December 1990, was followed by a hostile phone-in programme on Radio Lincolnshire, demonstrations against the market stall run by Mrs Townsend, a petition to the shop's landlord demanding its closure, and hate mail through the post. And because the insurers had not been informed of the hate campaign they have refused to meet the cost of the fire damage – estimated at £29,000. The business faces collapse not because of commercial failure or any legal or moral wrongdoing, but because certain 'Christians' chose to reject a central tenet of their religion: Love thy neighbour as thyself.

For Jill Simpson the campaign against her was even more unexpected and far more dreadful. It did not directly involve fundamentalists, but it was the product of persistent yet groundless assertions (which are examined in detail in Chapter 8) by fundamentalist 'authorities' that a wave of child abuse linked to satanic rituals was sweeping the United States. Her ordeal began in April 1989 with accusations that she had sexually abused a four-year-old pupil at the Breezy Point Day School, at Langhorne, Pennsylvania, where she worked. Within three months she was further accused of abusing two other young children, and by October the accusations against her had expanded to include her husband and sons as participants in animal sacrifice and sexual abuse as part of regular Satanic Masses. The accusing parents brought in a self-styled 'expert' on satanic abuse to support their case, and it was only eleven months of long and patient detective work that finally showed beyond any shadow of doubt that the accusations were nothing but child fantasies, and that Mrs Simpson and her family were completely innocent of all the charges against them. But she cannot bring herself to resume her teaching career; the Simpsons' home may have to be sold to meet the cost of their legal battle; and the Breezy Point Day School has suffered a significant decline in income.

Appalling though these cases are, they are not exceptional, nor do they exhaust the activities of fundamentalist opponents of the New Age. Particularly shocking, with its echoes of the Third Reich, is the urge towards burning books, records and tapes that are considered satanic. This is exemplified by the injunctions in various fundamentalist anti-masonic works to burn 'regalia, insignia and ritual books', and by the actions of Phil Day, a Pentecostalist Pastor of Boulder, Colorado, who in March 1988 burned such titles as Shirley MacLaine's *Out on a Limb* because they were 'demonic or symbolic of New Age thinking'. 'We were killing Satan,' said Mr Day. (*Boulder Daily Camera*, 15 March 1988.)

An appropriate judgement upon such actions was made by a high-school boy in Cincinnati in 1983. Encouraged by Billy Adams, an evangelist from Georgia, the members of the Community Pentecostal Church of God indulged in an orgy of record and tape burning: not just rock music, but 'even albums of Judy Collins' folk music, records by country stars Merle Haggard and Freddie Fender, and a couple of Mills Brothers albums were destroyed.' 'Rock music,' said Adams, 'is the devil's music.' To the high-school boy, however, 'This is barbaric. This is what the Nazis did. They're condemning a whole genre of music. It's insane.' (*Cincinnati Enquirer*, 5 March 1983.)

Insane it may be, but still it is done. At present the victims of fundamentalist intolerance are relatively few but, as we shall see, they continually grow in number. Of course, even if every New Age enthusiast, every alternative medical practitioner, every non-Christian worshipper in the land was under threat, the majority of the population would still be unaffected. Or would it? There are two dangers that tend to be overlooked.

One is that any restriction of the right to complete freedom (but not licence) in matters of religious worship and belief will inevitably lead to restrictions being imposed on all unorthodox spiritual practices, legally permissible and morally acceptable though they may currently be, and ultimately to an oppressive spiritual climate in which restrictions on religion will become arbitrary, placing the religious freedom of all – including the fundamentalists – in the same jeopardy.

The other danger is that uncritical hostility to the beliefs and actions of fundamentalists of whatever faith tends towards the acceptance of the right of any and every belief-system to unfettered propagation of its views and practices, however noxious these may be. This in turn leads, equally inevitably, to public hostility to all minority religions, whether extreme or not, and to the growth of a socio-political climate in which the repression of freedom of belief and expression is not only tolerated but is actively encouraged by a majority of the population.

Already there are signs of this second danger in the publicly expressed reactions, both in Britain and in North America, to the phenomenon of 'Political Correctness'. This vague 'movement' has grown out of a laudable desire to abolish from education, employment and every aspect of social and political life, all inequities based upon race, gender, ability and sexual inclination. But what ought to be the very epitome of religious and political tolerance has been diverted by fanatics into a movement to persecute those who espouse traditional religious and educational beliefs.

When the sometimes silly behaviour of devotees of 'P.C.' is reported in the mass media, public derision – and underlying hostility – are a certain consequence. It is difficult to envisage any other response to allowing Christmas trees on government property in America if they are considered pagan, but banning them if they are Christian, or to the banning of a nativity scene at Vienna, Virginia on the grounds that its presence on public land was 'unconstitutional' and would imply that the government was condoning 'religious symbolism'. Andrew Stephen, who reported this folly (*The Observer*, 29 December 1991), commented that this attitude to Christmas reflected 'America's frantic desire to be tolerant' – a desire so intense that 'it is turning into an intolerant country.'

And so it is, because imposed tolerance, however silly, can slide all too easily into intolerance and persecution, as with the case of Alan Gribben, a former lecturer in English at the University of Texas in Austin. Although a former student radical, Mr Gribben was, in 1991, condemned as a racist for voting against a new master's level programme in Third World and Minority literature, even though he did this to propose instead a doctoral programme. When he went on to protest that elevating material with a pronounced political slant to the left into required reading for an English composition course was subordinating instruction to indoctrination, he was subjected to a real and growing persecution. His departmental colleagues and students all ostracized him; he was bombarded with hate mail; and a campus rally publicly denounced him for 'racism'. Eventually he resigned and took up another teaching post in Alabama, driven out by a 'tolerance' that had progressed from undermining freedom of belief to an open attack on freedom of speech.

In Britain there are, as yet, no entrenched mechanisms whereby Political Correctness can carry persecution to such lengths. But there is no less venom in its devotees. After making threatening telephone calls to him, they attacked the home of Norman Stone, Professor of English at Oxford, who had, in 1991, criticized gay activists; while in Cambridge, John Casey, an English lecturer and Fellow of Gonville and Caius College, has also suffered. Because of an intemperate speech on West Indian immigration that he delivered in 1982, he has faced public vilification as a racist and 'latent fascist', and a student boycott of his lectures throughout 1991 – even though he has publicly, and often, repudiated the views he expressed nine years before. As with all versions of intolerance, Political Correctness is both unforgiving and unforgetting.

So, of course, will be the reaction to it. It is difficult to imagine anything more calculated to reinforce the very opinions that these egalitarian zealots seek to suppress, unless it be the dangerously misplaced tolerance of Dr George Carey, the present Archbishop of Canterbury. Speaking before the University of York in November 1991, Dr Carey urged his audience to understand Muslim distress at 'the outrageous slur on the Prophet' in Salman Rushdie's book, *The Satanic Verses*, which he likened to the distress that would have been felt by Christians if Scorsese's film, *The Last Temptation of Christ*, had been broadcast on British television. But he did not condemn, or even refer to, the *fatwah*, the sentence of death pronounced on Mr Rushdie in Iran and endorsed by many British Muslims. No literary insult, however hurtful, merits death threats; and no fear of the possible stirring of religious antagonisms should prevent a Christian (or any other) religious leader from condemning such threats.

Dr Carey's studied silence has achieved adverse public criticism. In a comment on his speech, the journalist Barbara Amiel wrote; 'If we tolerate cultures that put a bounty on the heads of our citizens, we cannot maintain a tolerant society.' (*The Sunday Times*, 1 December 1991.) A ringing phrase indeed, but it is not the whole of Islamic culture that is at fault in the Rushdie affair, merely a fanatical element within it. General hostility to Islam only serves to fuel the fires of religious hatreds. If we wish to prevent such fires we must steer a careful path between restrictions on religious behaviour (in its widest sense) and uncritical permissiveness as to its more bizarre manifestations.

If the free expression of widely differing beliefs and belief-systems is to be maintained, then those who hold them must accept that they have a responsibility to observe the general mores of the society in which they live; they must observe the established legal code of the country, and they must not set out deliberately to offend and outrage those whose beliefs differ from their own. This necessarily applies to fundamentalists as well as to those whose beliefs and behaviour they deplore, but lest it be thought that I seek to champion any and every unorthodox religious cult, or any specific manifestation of occultism and the New Age movement, I must make my own position clear.

I do not seek to proselytize on behalf of any denomination, movement or specific belief. I do not condone any action that is contrary to the law of the land, and I do not seek to endorse the specific beliefs, practices or social and spiritual attitudes of any individual, body or institution referred to in this study. But I do hold that every one of us has an inalienable right to choose his or her own set of social, philosophical and religious beliefs; to propagate those beliefs within the law; and to engage in whatever form of worship and lifestyle – again within the law of the land – they may imply.

That this right is currently under threat is, or ought to be, clear from the examples cited above, but to demonstrate this conclusively it is necessary to give many further instances of intolerance in action. There are, alas, all too many from which to choose, and as these are presented, it will be seen that injustice, immorality and illegality are variously displayed in all of them. In order fully to appreciate such examples, however, it is essential to understand something of the beliefs and practices involved; of the identity and motives of both the persecuted and their persecutors; and of a variety of technical terms that occur frequently in the text. All of this will require definitions and descriptions that are at once succinct, adequate and accurate – an almost impossible task that I do not pretend to have achieved to the satisfaction of all.

It is also necessary to expose the fear, the ignorance and, on occasion, the deliberate deceit that lies behind these examples of persecution in the name of faith. Only by replacing ignorance with knowledge, and deceit with the truth, will the fear be overcome. Only then will there be any hope that the persecutors might cease to persecute, and freedom of faith become a reality in our supposedly pluralist society.

ONE

Opposing Armies

Fundamentalist Christians and their sympathizers condemn and attack a very broad spectrum of beliefs and practices, almost always because they appear to fall foul of one or another biblical prohibition. But they rarely give precise, objective definitions of the various categories into which these beliefs and practices fall; indeed, they cannot do so because these definitions depend to such a large extent on the definer's personal prejudices. These categories are also somewhat elastic because their meaning has often subtly altered with the passage of time, and there is thus a considerable degree of overlapping and interlocking between them. Even so, reasonably crisp definitions are essential and I have tried to provide them in the second part of this chapter. It is, however, much easier to be objective when defining the various movements, groups and denominations within Christianity to which the attackers belong, or from which they dissent. It is also easier to gain a true understanding of their supposed opponents once their own nature and membership are properly understood.

Almost every denomination within the Christian Church accepts certain basic articles of faith: that there is only one God, the creator of all, who became human in the person of his son Jesus Christ; that Christ's teachings, which are contained in the four Gospels, are the authoritative guide to our faith and morals; that Christ died upon the Cross, but rose from the dead and ascended to the Father; that Christ's death atoned for the sins of mankind and made possible our salvation to eternal life; that God is present in the church in the person of the Holy Spirit; and that it is only through Christ that salvation can be attained.

There is also a general acceptance that the whole of the Bible, both Old and New Testaments, is the Word of God: an expression of his will, a record of his dealings with mankind, and a prophecy of man's future. But there is no universal consensus as to the degree to which the Bible should be considered divinely inspired and literally true, or as to how it should be interpreted; and most of the doctrinal differences that separate one denomination from another are due to disputes over biblical interpretation. Other causes of division have arisen from disputes over church organization, the manner of worship, and the authority of tradition and non-biblical writings.

Historically there have been two major rifts within Christianity. The first was in the eleventh century between the Eastern Church (Orthodox) and that of the West (Roman Catholic). This division was due in part to arguments over the precise definition of the doctrine of the Trinity (i.e. God as Father, Son and Holy Spirit), but even more to a dispute over the authority of the Pope, the Bishop of Rome. Five centuries later there came the Protestant Reformation, a movement in northern Europe seeking to reform the Church by rejecting papal authority and restoring the supremacy of the Bible over Church tradition.

By the end of the sixteenth century Protestantism had become, as it still is, the dominant form of Christianity in northern Europe, while Latin Europe remained Catholic. But both forms of Western Christianity are characterized by missionary zeal, and as the European nations built their empires, so they took either Protestant or Catholic Christianity with them. The pattern of religious allegiance then laid down – whether conversion was by coercion or conviction – has not greatly changed. Thus Latin America is now predominantly Catholic, while Protestant Churches are extremely strong in North America – although immigrants to the United States are so diverse in origin that no single Church holds a dominant position there.

This situation illustrates another significant difference between the Roman Catholic and Protestant Churches. The former is strongly hierarchical with a central authority dictating faith, morals, and forms of worship, while most Protestant Churches lay greater emphasis on a personal relationship with God and on the individual exercise of conscience. As a consequence, the Catholic Church has suffered few divisions, but new Protestant Churches, movements and sects have never ceased to arise, many of them being fervently evangelical in character. The members of such Churches tend to combine missionary zeal with a rigid fundamentalism that all too often results in conflict when they encounter the followers of other faiths. But what *is* 'fundamentalism'?

The essential feature of all fundamentalism is its unshakeable dogmatism. Within Christianity this has led to the term being applied loosely to all theological conservatism, although the term was originally applied specifically to the stance of a group of American Protestants who, in 1910, published a series of tracts – *The Fundamentals* – setting out the conservative theological position. Their aim was to oppose 'liberal' theology and to protect the essential, or fundamental, doctrines of the Christian faith from what they saw as the destructive effects of modern thought.

They maintained that true Christianity entails unquestioning belief that the whole of the Bible is divinely inspired, inerrant and literally true. If this is accepted, then other beliefs necessarily follow: the reality of the Virgin Birth, the miracles of Christ, and the Resurrection; the total depravity (or sinfulness) of Man, consequent upon the Fall as related in Genesis; the atonement of the sins of mankind through the sacrificial death of Christ; salvation through faith alone; the Second Coming of Christ before the Millennium as described in *Revelation*. In addition, fundamentalists accept uncritically the reality of eternal punishment and the active presence of supernatural evil powers in the world. They also emphasize the need for separation from unbelievers. The significance of this attitude and of these last beliefs will become increasingly clear as the tale of fundamentalist intolerance unfolds.

But not all conservative Christians are fundamentalists in any pejorative sense of the word. For many others, who readily accept the traditional Christian doctrines as set out in the New

Testament, the generic term 'evangelical' is more appropriate. They are equally as sure of those doctrines, for they emphasize the authority of the Bible which they accept as the divine rule of faith and practice. In this sense they *are* fundamentalists, but they differ from those to whom that label is commonly applied in that they take a less embattled view of their faith: because they see Christ as the only way to salvation, they seek to take the Gospel, the 'Good News' (*evangelion*), of the Christian faith to the world at large. But while the nature of their faith necessarily leads them to deny that ultimate truth is to be found outside Christianity, they do not seek to interfere with either the moral right of others to hold conflicting beliefs, or the free expression of such beliefs in the practice of non-evangelical or non-Christian worship. Nor do they deliberately avoid all association with non-believers. True fundamentalists often pay lip-service to freedom of belief, but in practice they are, as we shall see, of a far less tolerant stamp.

The combative approach to any public profession of a belief system that falls outside the narrow confines of conservative Protestantism tends to be associated with an exaggerated degree of religious enthusiasm. Such enthusiasm, which can all too easily be transformed into spiritual arrogance, is traditionally absent from the well-established Christian Churches which have become firmly integrated into society as a whole. It is more often associated with the Charismatic Movement – a movement which has, over the last thirty years, taken root in almost every traditional Christian denomination, and which continues to grow at a phenomenal rate.

Simply stated, the Charismatic Movement emphasizes the Gifts of the Holy Spirit: those spiritual abilities catalogued by Paul in his first letter to the Corinthians. They comprise the gifts of speaking words of wisdom and knowledge; of receiving faith; of the abilities to heal and to work miracles; to prophesy; to discern spirits; to speak ecstatically in unknown tongues; and to interpret such speech. Not all of these gifts are received by every Charismatic, and greater importance is placed on the Baptism in the Holy Spirit – a dramatic sudden awareness of the presence of the Holy Spirit, subsequent to a climactic conversion experience. It is often accompanied by 'speaking with tongues', but for Charismatics in the traditional Churches what is more important is the 'release of the Spirit' that had already been received at the believer's water baptism.

Historically, the movement began in the early years of this century and became institutionalized in the form of Pentecostal Churches (named after Pentecost, the Jewish feast day on which the Holy Spirit descended on the Apostles), the largest of which – the Assemblies of God – was founded in 1914. For many years the traditional denominations were uneasy with the phenomenon of 'speaking with tongues' and looked upon the Pentecostal Churches with some suspicion. But a more favourable attitude towards them has developed with the acceptance by the traditional Churches that for the foreseeable future, the Charismatic Movement, and all that it stands for, will play an increasingly significant role in their life and work.

For those favourably disposed towards it, the Movement is taken as a sign of 'renewal' within the Church, while for some the reappearance of supernatural Gifts of the Spirit is a sign that the Second Coming of Christ is imminent. This necessarily gives an urgency to their evangelizing and colours the attitudes of Charismatics to the religious behaviour of non-believers. It would, however, be wrong to suggest that all Charismatics are actively hostile to and intolerant of everyone who does not accept their beliefs. Equally it cannot be ignored that many of them are intolerant of non-believers. At which point we must consider just who are the Charismatics and why they practise this particular form of Christianity. We can then begin to understand what fuels their intolerance.

Before the Charismatic Movement grew up in the mainline denominations, the Pentecostal Churches in Britain and America drew most of their members from the ranks of the poor and the socially deprived. They offered religious absolutes and the certainty of a better life to come, as compared with the suffering and grinding poverty of everyday life – endorsing the guarantee with their ecstatic mode of worship. In Third World countries, where Pentecostalist Churches are undergoing spectacular growth, converts are still drawn almost exclusively from among the disaffected and dislocated poor. By way of contrast, the Charismatic Movement in Western society today is largely a middle class phenomenon. It has been argued that this is due to emotional insecurity arising from the cultural anonymity that increasingly affects the middle class. (D. Harrell, *All things are possible: The Healing and Charismatic Revivals in Modern America*, Indiana University Press, 1975.) Thus uncritical religious certainties that once brought solace to the materially poor now provide escape from spiritual poverty for the affluent.

There are no objective means of gauging the validity of specific conversion experiences (i.e. whether the individual has truly been 'Born again'), but it would be quite unjust to deny the religious sincerity of most Charismatics. There is, however, no dispute as to the socio-economic composition of the Charismatic Movement in general, nor of the commitment of its members to the cause: they are predominantly middle class and affluent, and willing to devote a large proportion of their disposable incomes to the service of their faith. One consequence of this financial strength has been the establishment and maintenance of many new Christian churches, fellowships and other bodies, founded by Charismatics (and occasionally by other fundamentalists) who have become dissatisfied with the apparent lack of religious fervour within the more staid traditional churches.

Typical of such 'new' organizations is a Baptist church at Bracknell, Berkshire, whose minister, the Reverend Ben Davies, was 'baptized in the spirit' twenty years ago and is now creating a huge 1,000-seat church centre at a cost of £3 million. It is funded entirely by his 600-strong congregation who are happy to give a tithe (a tenth) or even a 'double-tithe' of their incomes: in 1989 alone they donated £514,000. At Aldershot in Hampshire a former cinema has been converted into 'The King's Church' at a cost of £750,000 – raised by its members in less than five years. Its congregation now numbers over 1,000 and the annual turnover of the church is almost half a million pounds.

Much of that money is devoted to evangelism, for these churches do not work in isolation. Thus the Ichthus Fellowship (a group of thirty-one evangelical churches in south London and Surrey) paid £200,000 for the purchase and conversion of The Brown Bear, a public house in south London that now acts as a centre for bringing the faith to a previously impervious youth culture. Nor is missionary work in the Third World neglected, although political and religious restriction render such work difficult: evangelism is virtually impossible in Islamic countries and in mainland China. It thrives, however, in Latin America where there has been a marked swing away from traditional Roman Catholicism towards fundamentalist Protestantism. More than ten per cent of the population is now Protestant (with seventy per cent of that total being pentecostal), and in Brazil – the largest Catholic country in the world – half a million Catholics defect every year to Protestant Churches.

That such conversions may be fuelled by social despair is highly probable, but they are made possible only by the active presence of fundamentalist missionaries – paid for by their home congregations. And money that cannot usefully be channelled into overseas missionary work is expended on similar work at home: programmes of church building, and 'outreach' by way of publishing, propaganda, pop concerts, rallies and festivals. The aim is always the same: to convert a non-believing population to an uncompromising version of the Christian faith, with an absolute belief in the literal truth of the Bible and an absolute hostility to 'liberal' trends in social and sexual mores.

Such activities are certainly successful if the numbers of people involved are any guide. One of the largest fundamentalist festivals in Britain is the 'Spring Harvest' organized by the Evangelical Alliance. This interdenominational body was founded in 1846 to concentrate the strength of Protestants 'to promote the interests of a scriptural Christianity,' but its initial success was followed by slow decline until after World War Two when it sponsored Billy Graham's Crusades and began its work of media evangelism. Today the Alliance represents over one million evangelicals, and while it supports mutual action by evangelical Churches, dialogue with other Christian traditions is conditional upon there being no doctrinal compromise.

When the 'Spring Harvest' festival began in 1978, 2,700 people attended to celebrate the doctrinal and moral absolutism of their beliefs. By 1991 the festival had grown to over 70,000 celebrating in four holiday camps. An even more startling increase in numbers has been visible in the annual 'March For Jesus'. This interdenominational, evangelical event began in 1987 when 16,000 marched; by 1991 almost 250,000 took part – a local reflection of the phenomenal growth of fundamentalist Christianity around the world when traditional Church membership is in decline.

From 1979 to 1989 attendance at the mainstream Churches in Britain declined by between 9 per cent and 14 per cent, while in the same period the new independent Churches grew by 42 per cent. Similarly, figures in the 1991 *Yearbook of American and Canadian Churches* show that in 1989 conservative evangelical Churches in the USA continued to grow at the expense of other mainstream Churches. There are now some fifteen million fundamentalist Southern Baptists, while the Assemblies of God have over one million members (compared with less than half that number twenty years ago.)

As simple statistics these figures give no cause for alarm, for there have been continual shifts in religious allegiance since recorded history began. But together with their simplistic Christian faith the majority of fundamentalists display other characteristics which militate against tolerance in matters of belief. In general, fundamentalist Churches are anti-intellectual, in the sense that they are hostile to all critical examination of their own beliefs. Their attitude is neatly summarized by Morran and Schlemmer in their book, *Faith for the Fearful.* Although the passage quoted refers specifically to new, Charismatic Churches, its content is based on thorough sociological analysis, and can be applied with equal force to *all* fundamentalist denominations:

> Rational thinking, doubt and uncertainty are regarded either as demonic, or as avenues for Satan to penetrate human defences. Very little information apart from that which confirms the belief system of new church members is allowed to penetrate the discourse of the congregation. Most of the spare time of new church charismatic adherents is spent in church activities and most of their friends are also new church members. They tend to avoid going to the cinema and they tend to read only that which directly confirms their beliefs. This serves to encourage commitment but also

close-mindedness, fanaticism and inability to consider other points of view. (p. 176.)

The authors conclude on a sombre note: 'This attitude bodes badly for dialogue between churches or for attempts at ecumenicity.'

Fundamentalists do not like and, for the most part, do not participate in the ecumenical movement, which aims at recovering 'the unity of all believers in Christ, transcending differences of creed, ritual and polity.' It threatens a dilution of 'pure' doctrine, and would necessarily lead to links with Churches that many fundamentalists consider to be apostate: the Roman Catholic, Orthodox, and American Episcopalian Churches being prime examples. Thus they have no truck with the World Council of Churches, nor with equivalent national bodies. Their rejection of ecumenism is best illustrated from the USA, where in 1987 some 60 per cent of Protestants – one third of all American Christians – were in conservative denominations that shun the National Council of Churches of Christ in America.

But who are the Christians whom fundamentalists reject? Apart from the Roman Catholic Church which has traditionally been seen as an enemy, fundamentalist venom is reserved especially for liberal Protestant theologians who do not look upon the Bible as wholly divinely inspired, nor as literally true. The very idea of subjecting the Bible to critical analysis on historical, archaeological, linguistic, textual and philosophical grounds is anathema to the fundamentalist. Theologians who do so, and who question specific doctrines as a consequence, are condemned – as, it might be added, they have been similarly condemned by conservatives within the Roman Catholic Church.

Christians who are prepared to enter into dialogue with those of other faiths, or who see merit in alternative medicine, in concern for the environment, and in any aspect of the New Age movement are similarly condemned. For the fundamentalist there can be no fellowship between light and darkness and, for him, all that falls outside his narrow field of vision is of the darkness. It is also necessarily evil, something to be fought against and to overcome.

At the 'Spring Harvest' festival at Skegness, Lincolnshire, in 1990, the Evangelical Alliance organized a seminar on the occult in the course of which Faith Forster – one of the founders of the Ichthus Fellowship – offered the following prayer:

> I pray, Lord, that you will forgive me for my interest in occult activity. I ask, Lord, that you will cleanse me from all the effects of that occult activity. Deliver me from the Evil One now, in Jesus' name. Amen! And now, Lord, we come against all these things! We break the power of witchcraft, freemasonry and every evil practice! (Ian Cotton, 'Share it Brother' in *Sunday Times Magazine*, 1990.)

Several points are implicit in this prayer:

1. 'occult activity' is evil;
2. it is associated with Satan, the Evil One;
3. a social organization, Freemasonry, is associated with witchcraft and un-named 'evil practices'.

No justification is given for any of this but, as we shall see, fundamentalists will readily supply one if called on to do so. In essence, however, these 'evil practices' are any activity directly or indirectly associated with the New Age. Which brings us to the New Age itself.

The term 'New Age' has been too loosely applied, too often, to far too many widely differing practices, beliefs and disciplines for it to be given any precise definition that is universally acceptable. We can, indeed, sympathize with the fundamentalist critic Michael Cole when he writes of the New Age that 'It is far easier to describe than to define'. (*What is the New Age?* p.5.) The description he gives is both unkind and unjust, but it typifies the fundamentalist attitude:

> It is an inclusive and syncretistic movement, tolerant of all except the exclusive and distinctive claims of both the Jewish and Christian revelations. It can be likened to a religious octopus whose tentacles reach out to all who attempt to satisfy the spiritual needs of men. It is a rag-bag embracing the cults, the occult, Hinduism, freemasonry, theosophy and astrology, among other movements. (p.6.)

Constance Cumbcy, one of the most influential and widely read of fundamentalist self-styled 'experts' on the New Age, defines it as 'a worldwide coalition of networking organizations. It also includes individuals bound together by common mystical experiences.' (*The Hidden Dangers of the Rainbow*, p.247.) She goes on to gather under this umbrella almost every body of which fundamentalists disapprove. Others are somewhat less vague: for Walter Martin, founder of the Christian Research Institute, the 'New Age Cult . . . can be equated with the transplantation of Hindu philosophy through the Theosophical Society'. (*The New Age Cult*, p.15.) But, as with Mrs Cumbey, he goes on to link it with other 'questionable' movements, notably those concerned with the environment and with holistic medicine.

Advocates of the New Age are often equally vague. Eileen Campbell describes 'New Age' as:

> an 'umbrella term' that is used to denote a whole range of interests including health and well-being, the many forms of therapy or self-help, the practice of an esoteric or spiritual tradition, concern for the rest of humanity and the environment, and respect for Nature and feminine wisdom. (Campbell and Brennan, *The Aquarian Guide to the New Age*, p.7.)

By way of contrast, John Cornwell's brief definition of the New Age as a 'loose alliance of spiritual quests' (*Powers of Darkness, Powers of Light*, p.351) comes as a welcome relief. His expanded description is admirable, and from it one can pluck clear pointers to the nature of the New Age and begin to discern just why it is so abhorrent to the fundamentalist. 'New Ageism,' he states:

> is a focus for the view that human beings are approaching another stage of evolution by discovering alternative powers within themselves, within the planet and cosmos'.

Central to the movement is the concept of holism,

> the notion that mind, body and spirit, all the systems of the planet and cosmos, must be seen as a whole, seen in terms of multi-relationships.

And here we come to the unbridgeable chasm between New

Age beliefs and fundamentalist Christianity. The 'New Ageist' frowns upon dogma and regards Christ 'as merely another "evolved master"'. He does not condemn Christianity but looks upon it merely as 'one of many means to achieve the promise of a wholly new approach to spiritual consciousness and practice'. And just as the New Ageist is indifferent to Christianity, so he is to orthodox science: 'the insights and efficacies of Eastern philosophies, alternative technologies and healing arts, are deemed superior to most reductionist Western science and medicine.' As we shall see, this heinous indifference by the New Age movement leads fundamentalists into an unlikely and uneasy alliance with materialist scientists to further their persecution.

But what of occultism and the other cults, movements and activities in Michael Cole's 'rag-bag' and in Mrs Forster's prayer? In almost every case fundamentalist beliefs about them are grounded in ignorance, mixing reality with fantasy and truth with error. These confused beliefs then percolate through the general public via an equally ignorant popular press that has never been noted for putting truth before sensation. Objective descriptions will not sweep away fundamentalist suspicion and hostility, but they may provide some ground for constructive dialogue, and they will certainly help the neutral observer.

Before dealing with specifics we should consider sects and cults. Both words are scattered wholesale by fundamentalists (and others) as terms of vilification, but what are they? A *cult* may be defined as any religious group which differs significantly in one or more respects as to belief or practice from those religious groups which are regarded as the normative expressions of religion in the culture within which it exists. It does not necessarily derive from the prevailing religion of that culture, whereas a *sect* is a breakaway religious body; especially one that is regarded as extreme, intolerant, or exclusive by the larger group from which it has separated. Thus fundamentalists are justified in considering some aspects of the New Age movement as cults, but it does not follow that because a given body is correctly styled a cult its nature is necessarily unwholesome.

Here I must insert a caveat. It must not be supposed that

I am in any way seeking to propagate the beliefs and practices of specific cults. Their activities are often such that one can readily sympathize with those who object to them; indeed, I find many of them distasteful and would be happy to see them fade away. But as long as adult cult members neither break the law of the land nor encourage others to do so, they have a right to believe what they wish and to worship as they choose. No personal distaste we may feel for them should lead us to ignore those rights or to break the law ourselves.

After the precision of 'cult', occultism is a more difficult term to pin down. The word 'occult' simply means 'hidden', but occultism has been defined (Nandor Fodor, *Encyclopaedia of Psychic Science*) as 'a philosophical system of theories and practices on, and for the attainment of, the higher powers of mind and spirit. Its practical side connects with psychical phenomena.' This, of course, begs the question as to the reality of such 'higher powers', and does not refer to the implicit secrecy of such theories and practices. Fundamentalists admit the reality of the 'higher powers', but emphasize the secrecy of occultism and claim that the source of its practices is demonic.

Historically the term 'occultism' is of comparatively recent origin, first occurring in English in 1877 (in Madame Blavatsky's *Isis Unveiled*), and what fundamentalists attack is more properly labelled the 'occult sciences'; that is, those practices, 'called transcendental and magical, a knowledge of which has been transmitted and accumulated in secret, or is contained in books that have an inner or secret meaning'. (Waite, *The Occult Sciences*, p.v). Which brings us to magic.

In brief, magic is the art that purports to control or forecast natural events, effects, or forces by invoking the supernatural. For its practitioners it is a means of expanding awareness to supposed 'higher' levels of being by working carefully structured, complex rituals that involve the invocation of supernatural forces. They perceive magic as morally neutral; whether it is good or evil depends on the purpose to which it is put. For the fundamentalist, all meddling with supernatural forces is evil.

From this point of view, all psychic phenomena and any organized attempt to make contact with the spirits of the dead are equally evil. Thus spiritualism, the belief that the dead can communicate with the living through the agency of a person (a medium) who is gifted with the appropriate ability, is condemned by fundamentalists. When this belief is elevated to the status of a religion with distinctive doctrines and forms of worship it is anathema.

All of this tends to be labelled by the fundamentalist, rightly or wrongly, as 'occultism', and the same label is often applied to other quite specific practices and beliefs. A prime example is 'witchcraft', an emotive word whose meaning varies widely according to the context of its use. Historically it referred to the practice of black magic or sorcery (the words tend to be interchangeable outside the realm of anthropology); that is, the manipulation of natural forces, animals and human beings by supernatural means, and with the aid of evil spirits, for selfish and wicked ends. It was taken as axiomatic that the witch (who could be male or female) had renounced Christianity and sworn allegiance to the devil. But the theory had no basis in reality. Not one of the thousands of recorded trials for witchcraft in Europe and North America (mostly during the sixteenth and seventeenth centuries) produced objective evidence of any wrong doing, or of any of the supposed practices of witchcraft. The evil lay in the accusers and in the judicial systems that perpetuated such a monstrous fantasy.

Unfortunately for the fundamentalist peace of mind, a wayward anthropologist, Margaret Murray, propounded in 1921 the theory that witchcraft was a reality, but that it represented the survival of pre-Christian religious practices. No historian and no other anthropologist has ever accepted her theory (for which no historical evidence exists), but in 1954 an English occultist, Gerald Gardner, claimed that this pre-Christian religion still existed, giving it a theology and form of worship derived in equal measure from Victorian occultism and his own fertile imagination. His new religion took instant root and has flourished ever since under the name of Wicca (the Old English for a male witch). Its harmless followers seek to revive a more-or-less Celtic paganism, redesigned to harmonize with modern urban society. They are essentially indifferent to Christianity, but the open hostility of fundamentalists towards them has led some witches to deride Christianity – thus fuelling the spiral of hatred and encouraging yet further persecution.

Witches may accept the label of pagans, in that they do not follow either Christianity or any other major world religion, but adhere instead to a creed based upon presumed pre-Christian Western religious beliefs and more recent 'occult' practices, but they bitterly resent being styled 'Satanists'. Logically they should not be accused of Satanism, for this is the worship of the supernatural power which Judaism and Christianity both regard as the origin of evil; those who do not accept the reality of Satan cannot worship him.

In practice Satanism is, and always has been, of rare occurrence. The majority who profess to being Satanists are not so much consciously espousing spiritual evil as seeking to throw off the shackles of conventional morality in a manner that emphasizes their social and psychological immaturity. Whether they are seen as extreme hedonists or as perverts, their principal motivation appears to be the pursuit of sexual licence. There is no evidence outside the realms of overt fiction and fantasy that any self-styled Satanist has ever succeeded in gaining material wealth and power through the worship of Satan.

The smear of Satanism has also been applied to Freemasonry. This is especially unjust as Freemasonry is not a religion, and the majority of Freemasons in England and America are professing Christians or Jews. It is a worldwide secular, fraternal society, open to men of good repute of all races and religions who believe in God. Although it is neither a religion nor a substitute for religion, it is concerned with spiritual values that underpin the orthodox tenets of private and public morality that are instilled in its members. It teaches these moral precepts through a series of ritual dramas (largely based on biblical stories, especially the legends surrounding the building of King Solomon's Temple) that use the customs and tools of the medieval stonemasons as allegorical guides. Although it has always been strictly apolitical and non-sectarian, the accidents of history have led some Freemasons into political actions that have earned the enmity of both Church and State. Because of this, and because masonic meetings are strictly private, the most bizarre fantasies concerning Freemasonry have been bandied about and are still taken for truth by fundamentalists today.

Similar fantasies abound concerning the Rosicrucians, who have been historically linked with Freemasonry, but many of these are propagated by self-styled Rosicrucians themselves. Technically the name should be applied only to those bodies whose beliefs and practices are based on the three Rosicrucian Manifestos of the early seventeenth century. These concern the life and teachings of the mythical Christian Rosenkreutz, a Protestant mystic who allegedly founded a quasi-monastic Order dedicated to healing the sick (by means that would now be considered as alternative therapies), and propagating Christian doctrines in allegorical, usually alchemical and astrological, guise. The name has since been taken up by groups that are not restricted to Christian beliefs and that incorporate many of the more fanciful ideas of nineteenth century occultism, especially those promoted by the Theosophical Society.

If it had remained rigidly true to its objects, the Theosophical Society would not have promoted any specific ideas, but its founders, Colonel Olcott and Madame H.P. Blavatsky, were intent on bringing 'Theosophy', their version of oriental wisdom, to the West and promoting it as absolute truth. Madame Blavatsky's work – a curious jumble of Eastern, Western and Classical pagan religious concepts – is also coloured by her hostility to institutional Christianity. This stance, coupled with a similar anti-Christian animus on the part of her successor, Annie Besant, aroused the especial and lasting ire of fundamentalists. But it need never have been so. The Society has never held corporate views and its stated objects effectively preclude all dogmatic statements. They are: to form a nucleus of the universal brotherhood of humanity without distinction of race, creed, sex, caste or colour; to encourage the study of comparative religion, philosophy and science; and to investigate unexplained laws of nature and the powers latent in man. These objects may not greatly appeal to fundamentalists, but there is nothing in them to excite Christian condemnation.

Also subject to fundamentalist disapproval are all forms of divination – especially astrology, because of its seemingly all-pervasive influence. Depending on one's point of view, astrology is a science or an art, involving the study of the relative positions of the sun, moon and planets against the background of the stars, in the belief that they exert an influence upon humanity, and that from their positions at a given time it is possible to assess individual human characteristics, and to predict the potential course of human affairs. Other forms of divination make their assessments and predictions on the basis of numbers; the lines on the palm of the hand; the fall of tossed coins; the random layout of playing cards or Tarot cards; and an enormous number of other variables. Whether or not there is any validity in any of these systems is still a disputed question, but this is irrelevant for the fundamentalist, for whom it is sufficient to bask in the certain knowledge that God has condemned such practices.

Even this does not exhaust the catalogue of seemingly damnable practices. Holistic medicine and the therapies it offers as alternatives to surgery and allopathic medicine (the use of drugs to alleviate disease symptoms) are looked upon with suspicion. This is due in no small part to guilt by association. Thus homoeopathy – the treatment of disease by administering minute quantities of substances that in large doses would produce symptoms similar to those of the disease – is condemned because of its connection with the ideas of both Paracelsus and Swedenborg, as are the Bach Flower Remedies and Schuessler's Tissue Salts. Herbalism smacks of paganism; hypnosis is too closely linked with psychic phenomena; while yoga and other techniques of meditation and relaxation are tainted with Hinduism and other oriental religions.

And with such hostility to 'natural' remedies it is not surprising that fundamentalism is equally hostile to many aspects of the Ecological Movement. It would be wrong to claim that fundamentalists have no concern for the environment, for they live in the world and view the damage inflicted upon it by man-made pollution with as much anxiety as their non-believing neighbours. But many supporters of 'Green' political parties, of Greenpeace, of Friends of the Earth, and of similar environmentally concerned bodies tend also to support alternative therapies and other manifestations of the New Age. They are also usually on the left of the political spectrum whereas the majority of fundamentalist Christians favour political conservatism because it more closely reflects their own world view.

It also supports fundamentalist opposition to alternative lifestyles and to any movements in society that may be perceived as threatening the traditional structure of the family. But the interaction of political and religious intolerance is not a simple matter – it involves opportunism as much as conviction – and it will be addressed elsewhere in the text where discussion of its complexities is more appropriate. What is of more immediate concern is to consider the purpose of attacks upon alternative beliefs and religious practices. What motivates fundamentalists and what are their aims? And how do they justify their intolerance?

TWO

War Of The Saints

'We wrestle not against flesh and blood,' wrote Saint Paul
to the Ephesians (6:12), 'but against principalities, against
powers, against the rulers of the darkness of this world, against
spiritual wickedness in high places.' And this is the key to the
paradox of those supposedly Christian fundamentalists who
choose not to obey Christ's injunction to love their neighbours
as themselves, but to rage at their fellow human beings who
do not believe as they believe. For the fundamentalist there
can be no pity and no love in his ceaseless war against other
faiths and their false doctrines; because it is not simply a war
against those who profess such beliefs, but a ceaseless struggle
against the beliefs themselves and their ultimate source – it is
a crusade against Satan.

It also has the authority of the Word of God, which, for the
fundamentalist, is the sole and sovereign justification, both
necessary and sufficient. For the believer in its inerrancy the
Bible is a rich mine for texts with which to beat his opponents
about the ears. Biblical authority is also cited in a general
sense, especially to vindicate the points of view expressed in
the many letters to the national and local press that stress the
need to fight occultism and the New Age in general. Thus the
author of a letter to the *Bristol Evening Post* (9 February 1990),
condemning the Bristol Psychic Fair, simply stated that 'these
practices are an abomination to God, who forbids people to
indulge in them'. Had it been demanded he would certainly
have provided the appropriate chapter and verse, but specific

text quotation is largely reserved for the faithful, either for declamation from the pulpit, or for the unending stream of books and pamphlets that attack all things 'occult'.

The use, or rather abuse, of biblical texts taken out of context has always been a part of religious controversy, but in the attacks on the New Age, on the New Religious Movements and on non-Christian beliefs in general it serves a dual purpose. In part it serves as a cudgel to belabour the enemy – although it is a somewhat futile blow given that the 'enemy' is unlikely to accept the authority of the Bible – and, more importantly, it also helps to reinforce the rigid belief system and prejudices of those who read, believe and act upon the contents of the books in question and listen to the preaching of their authors.

In general, texts from the Old Testament are used more often than New Testament passages, and where the latter are used they are most often drawn from the Pauline Epistles: the words of the vengeful God of Saint Paul and the Hebrew prophets is invariably more appropriate than those of the loving and forgiving Jesus Christ. It would, however, be unfair to impute deliberate selectivity to the fundamentalists as, for them, any book of the Bible is as absolutely true as any other, and any text that will serve is thus considered wholly appropriate. What is alarming is the extent to which secular authorities are prepared to believe in the evil of occultism when a biblical warrant for condemning it is the only justification offered.

Among the most frequently cited texts is Deuteronomy 18:10–12

> There shall not be found among you any one who burns his son or daughter as an offering, any one who practises divination, a soothsayer, or an augur, or a sorcerer, or a charmer, or a medium, or a wizard, or a necromancer. For whoever does these things is an abomination to the Lord; and because of these abominable practices the Lord your God is driving them out before you.

Earlier in the same chapter is the command that any believer who has 'gone and served other gods and worshipped them, or the sun or the moon or any of the host of heaven, which I have forbidden' (17:3) is to be stoned to death. This, however, tends to be glossed over – perhaps because the civil law would not today look kindly on anyone, even a 'born again' Christian, who killed a lapsed church member who had taken up astrology.

Nor is Exodus 22:18 ('Thou shalt not suffer a witch to live') used as often today as it was when witchcraft was a capital crime. Perhaps it would encourage too many to read the Book of Exodus with care, and thus learn how God (through Moses) recognized slavery, commanded that 'Whoever strikes [or even curses] his father or his mother shall be put to death' (21:15 and 17), and ordered many other courses of action that no civilized society would now tolerate. That some fundamentalists would welcome the return of capital, or at least corporal, punishment is implicit in their writings. Thus Roy Livesey, a prolific author of works attacking the New Age, is clearly dismayed at the prospect that parents might lose the right to smack their children – although in fairness one should add that he sees this as part and parcel of the Satanic destruction of family life advocated by the United Nations. (*Understanding the New Age*, p.27.)

Many other texts are quoted from the Old Testament as they seem appropriate. They are rarely quoted in context, however, and it is instructive to read them in their proper setting: those who cite them with approval are likely to become extremely uncomfortable when faced with some of the injunctions contained in surrounding verses. Thus, Leviticus 19:31 contains this command: 'Do not turn to mediums or wizards; do not seek them out, to be defiled by them: I am the Lord your God.' In the following chapter (20:27) there is more: 'A man or a woman who is a medium or a wizard shall be put to death; they shall be stoned with stones, their blood shall be upon them.' If they were truly consistent, fundamentalists would be busy advocating the killing of most of those who advertise in the columns of such journals as *Psychic News* and *Prediction* (which slaughter would also conflict with God's command, 'Thou shalt not kill'; but consistency has never been a fundamentalist's strongpoint).

The story of Saul and the Witch – more properly a medium – of Endor in the First Book of Samuel (28) is divorced from its historical setting and used as a general cautionary tale to dissuade those who might be tempted to visit fortune-tellers.

Similarly Daniel (2) derides the failure of the 'wise men, enchanters, magicians or astrologers' correctly to interpret Nebuchadnezzar's dream, and his words are now used to justify a general opposition to astrology.

In the New Testament three texts are especially favoured. From the Second Epistle to the Corinthians is taken the justification for exclusivity: 'Do not be mismated with unbelievers. For what partnership have righteousness and iniquity? Or what fellowship has light with darkness? What accord has Christ with Belial? Or what has a believer in common with an unbeliever? . . . Therefore come out from them and be separate from them, says the Lord.' (6:14–17.) This is doubly valuable to the fundamentalist; on the one hand it is used to justify the absolute rejection of anything that might remotely be labelled as 'pagan' or 'occult', while on the other it justifies his shunning of any person who might be so labelled and thus enables him to avoid the risk of painful shock from a rational dialogue and examination of evidence.

But this Pharisaic injunction (supported by quotations from the Old Testament) applies specifically to mixed marriages, although it can be read in a more general sense. If it is, then it must be read as an absolute: Christians should not contaminate themselves by *any* contact with unbelievers. We might thus be justified in expecting those fundamentalists – and they are many – who quote it with approval, to avoid every shop, school, hospital, social centre, library or government office that is owned, staffed or administered by any but 'born again' Christians. Of course they do nothing of the sort, for that would render everyday life intolerable.

More liberal Christians are disposed of by means of another text from the same letter (11:12–15). This warns against 'false apostles . . . disguising themselves as apostles of Christ'. Clearly these are the critics of a literal interpretation, for the fundamentalist himself cannot be in error. He has also another text of crucial importance. In the Gospel according to John (14:6), Christ says of himself, 'I am the way, and the truth, and the life; no one comes to the Father, but by me.' All Christians necessarily believe this to be true, but they do not set limits on the way in which Christ may be known: only fundamentalists are so presumptuous. For non-Christians, of course, Christ's statement will carry no more weight than any other which they choose not to believe – and yet for the fundamentalist it is a justification for attempting to impose his faith on others.

There is in this an element of self-justification, for in one sense fundamentalists are analogous to an ethnic minority in an alien and hostile land. However they have arrived at their specific theological position, fundamentalists can identify with each other and perceive the larger world as the 'enemy'. This view of the structure of fundamentalism has been succinctly described by G. Marsden, in *Fundamentalism and American Culture* (Oxford University Press, 1980).

> Faced by a culture with a myriad of competing ideals, and having little power to influence that culture, they reacted by creating their own equivalent of the urban ghetto. An over-view of fundamentalism reveals them building a sub-culture with institutions, mores and social connections that would eventually provide acceptable alternatives to the dominant cultural ethos. (p.204.)

As long as fundamentalists continued to see themselves as an embattled minority, struggling against the world, the flesh and the devil, they were content for the outside world to be as 'pagan' as it wished to be. But as that outside world becomes more uncertain of itself, so the fundamentalist turns from being defensive to being aggressive: it is both his right and his duty to impose his mores upon others, whether or not they share his beliefs. The biblical code by which he lives tells him that he must reject a pluralist society, but as he must live in the world it is that pluralist society which must change. He knows that Christ came to save mankind, and so he must be thrust upon all men for their own good. All other beliefs must be cast aside.

But what sort of people are fundamentalists? There is no definitive sociological analysis of fundamentalism in Britain, and in its absence speculation is of little value; it also involves the risk of drawing too many unwarranted conclusions when considering the question of how to deal with fundamentalist intolerance. Certainly the Charismatic Movement is a largely middle-class phenomenon, but it is not confined to any one class within society, and the term 'middle-class' has now so broadened in its popular interpretation as to have little value save when considering the financial underpinning of fundamentalism. Nor is it necessarily true that British fundamentalists are drawn from the same broad social groups as in America, for similar social conditions do not apply – as is also true for different parts of the USA: the bulk of conservative Protestants are in the southern and mid-western States, where social attitudes are very different from those of the industrial north and the traditionally liberal north-east. Even so, it is not unreasonable to expect to find in Britain attitudes of mind and political sympathies analogous to those of fundamentalists in the United States.

In general, American conservative Protestants are also politically conservative; hostile to the perceived 'atheistic communism' of the former Soviet Union and its allies; opposed to the concept of a welfare state; and suspicious of any social innovation that can be seen as state interference with individual rights or with the maintenance of the nuclear family as the essential basis of Western society. There is, however, a perceived distinction between evangelicals and fundamentalists, in that the former are more likely to become politically involved and to become activists in movements related to contentious social issues. Fundamentalists, especially those in the Charismatic Movement, are more inward looking. Their attitudes are summed up by Morran and Schlemmer:

> The new churches are avowedly apolitical, claiming that the mission of the church is purely the saving of souls. The responsibilities of individual Christians are to live a Godly life and to spread the Gospel. Living a Godly life and spreading the Gospel do not include involvement in broader social or political issues. (*Faith for the Fearful*, p.13.)

Their biblical justification for rejecting the 'social gospel' is drawn from the Epistle to the Romans (13:1–2):

> Let every person be subject to the governing authorities. For there is no authority except from God, and those that exist have been instituted by God. Therefore he who resists the

authorities resists what God has appointed, and those who resist will incur judgment.

From this it necessarily follows that if the civil authorities should ever seek to suppress 'alternative' or minority beliefs and practices, they will receive the full support of fundamentalists – and of all other biblical literalists who may be presumed to subscribe to the same doctrine.

The social attitudes of both fundamentalists and other religious conservatives was made clear in the USA with the rise of the New Christian Right at the beginning of the Reagan presidency. The term applies less to specific institutions – although it was epitomized by the Moral Majority Movement of the Reverend Jerry Falwell, which demonstrated that, when united, religious conservatives could wield real political power – than to a set of underlying attitudes. These can be summed up as a hostility to 'secular humanism', the term by which American fundamentalists described the liberal attitudes underpinning the whole spectrum of social and cultural changes of which they disapproved.

These stemmed, or so it seemed to them, from the increasing interference of the State in social affairs, giving rise to monstrous growths: the rise of strident feminism; the breakdown of traditional family role models; the establishment of legal rights for minority racial and sexual groups; the liberalizing of attitudes to sex and the growth of pornography; and the increased use of abortion that was perceived as the worst consequence of all this.

The many organizations that now campaign on specific issues within this spectrum, such as the anti-abortion group, Operation Rescue, are largely dependent upon fundamentalists (using the term in its broad sense) for their membership. What is most worthy of remark – and perhaps of alarm – is that they increasingly include Roman Catholic fundamentalists. The state of mind that produces such religious attitudes is not limited to Protestant believers.

But for all their sound and fury they have so far had little effect on legislation in America concerning social issues nor influence on the outcome of national elections. This is not a cause for complacency, however, as is clear from the conclusions drawn by two observers of their role in the 1980 American presidential elections:

> The real importance of the Moral Majority and other New Christian Right organizations is not in what they accomplished during the 1980 elections, but in the *potential* they represent as a burgeoning social movement . . . There is much restlessness and discontent in America today, and much of it is mobilizable in the name of Christian virtue. (J. K. Hadden and C. E. Swann, *Primetime Preachers: The Rising Power of Televangelism*, Reading, Pa., 1981. Quoted in S. Bruce, *Pray TV. Televangelism in America*, 1990.)

During the last decade that restlessness and discontent has increased and is also visible in Britain. It helps to provide a growing reservoir of untapped frustration among fundamentalists. And because the New Age and alternative religions have fewer champions than do liberal causes, they provide an easier outlet for the frustration and hostility of the New Christian Right. They have also provided more fertile soil for the planting of restrictive legislation.

The political attitudes held by fundamentalists may thus be clear in broad terms, but knowing what they are does not answer the basic question of why religious extremism is a growing phenomenon within relatively liberal Western cultures. It is a problem that has been addressed only in broad terms and any answers must, for the present, be tentative. Perhaps it is best to consider first how fundamentalists fit into categories defined by the motives behind their beliefs.

Constructing such categories in the absence of statistical analyses is necessarily a subjective affair, but I would propose three major divisions.

First is that containing the 'true believers'; that is, those who sincerely and deeply believe that their approach to Christianity is the only true and viable way. Their dogmatic beliefs will lead them to maintain a total hostility to all that smacks of the 'occult', the New Age, or non-Christian faith. But because they have chosen their own beliefs freely and without internal or external psychological pressure, there is the constant hope that they will admit to holding false notions about other belief systems when faced with facts in place of fictions. From this may come a degree of tolerance that will permit a truce – or at least an armed neutrality – with those who dissent from their views.

Tolerance is less likely from those who have undergone a dramatic 'conversion' experience, whether they have been 'born again' and have left a more traditional branch of Christianity or converted from a non-Christian faith, or from some form of 'occult' belief. It is from this last group that many of those who fall into the more contentious second category are drawn. Those within it are at once more troubled and more troublous. They are the individuals who are drawn to fundamentalism by reason of personal fears and anxieties, by their own psychological inadequacy, or by psycho-spiritual problems that may include psychological disturbance of a pathological nature. They are also a major factor in propagating the many myths and distortions that surround the fundamentalist picture of the New Age. As they externalize their own fantasies, delusions and hallucinations, so they project them on to the church, movement, sect or belief which they have left behind.

The final group is quite different, and before they are considered it will be as well to look at the whole question of ignorance regarding the New Age and all associated with it. However the fundamentalist may have come by his faith, he is unlikely to be familiar with objective studies of the New Age or of any 'alternative' or non-Christian belief. As has already been pointed out, a fundamentalist tends to read only that which serves to confirm his own beliefs; and to inform himself about the New Age – and to confirm its demonic nature – he will turn to the vast range of books and pamphlets designed to reinforce all his existing prejudices. He is unlikely to seek out and study any objective works on such subjects.

Assuming, that is, that there *are* any. All too much of the literature from within the New Age movement, is imprecise; too all-embracing and unsubstantiated as to detail to be of real value when seeking to define beliefs or to discover their philosophical and historical sources. A random sample of entries from *The Aquarian Guide to the New Age* – Blake, Blavatsky, Cathars, Eckhart, Freemasonry, Golden Dawn,

Magic, Mysticism, Pagan, Qabalist, Secret Doctrine; the list could be almost endless – reveals them to be variously inaccurate, misleading, vague and inadequate. And this is selected not to criticize the authors, but because it is typical of modern works in this field; it is recent and readily obtainable, and it is respected within the confines of the New Age.

Should the fundamentalist venture to seek the literature of his 'enemies' it is not surprising that many of his fears are thus confirmed. Of course reliable works do exist but they rarely appeal to the popular mind for they puncture the myths of both sides. Which leads to the matter of a possible common source of both resurgent fundamentalism and the burgeoning New Age.

The Charismatic revival within mainline churches began in earnest in the 1960s, the quintessential decade of 'Youth Revolt'. The search for alternatives to staid, orthodox beliefs and lifestyles led to an upsurge of enthusiasm for dynamic expressions of worship, whether Christian or non-Christian. For some, perhaps more determined in their revolt against orthodoxy, this led to occultism and to the whole kaleidoscope of beliefs and practices that constitutes the New Age. For others, the road led to ecstatic worship within Christianity – to the immediacy of the pentecostal form of religious experience. There are clear parallels between both paths. Neither requires questioning or proof of the beliefs involved; there is a powerful psychic element in both (altered states of consciousness in the New Ager, and access to divine healing and other Gifts of the Spirit for the charismatic fundamentalist).

It must be admitted that the two paths represent different sets of value judgements, but the same yearning for a spiritual reality that seemed absent from everyday life underlies both. The New Ager is admittedly more syncretistic, his beliefs more amorphous than the fundamentalist but there is a markedly similar desire for religious certainty, and close parallels in the psycho-spiritual mechanisms involved in obtaining exalted religious experiences for both. For example, modern popular music exercises its appeal to youth irrespective of belief; rock music, which is essentially derived from the forms of negro Spirituals and the rhythms of Gospel music, is taken up with equal enthusiasm by Charismatic and New Ager alike as an aid to exaltation. The fundamentalist will, of course, reject the parallel as false – the teachers and deities of the New Age are seen, at best, as the 'False Apostles' against whom Saint Paul warned the Corinthians. And he will find his perception reinforced by what he reads, for there is hardly a book on the New Age, on 'occultism' or on alternative beliefs from within the fundamentalist and evangelical camps that is not in some way seriously flawed by the ignorance of its author.

This is a sweeping and serious charge, but one that can, alas, be all too easily proven. Many specific errors of fact – and examples of deliberate distortions and deceit – will be presented throughout subsequent chapters as the occasion demands, but a few samples must be given here to justify the charge. Let us begin with historical fantasies and consider what has been written about the Cathars, those morally impeccable dualists of the thirteenth century who were such a thorn in the flesh of the corrupt Church of the day.

The Cathars do not feature prominently in British fundamentalist works, but they are regularly condemned in America. For Pat Pulling (in *The Devil's Web*) they were a 'group frequently associated with early devil worship' (p.145), and they derived their name 'from the term 'cat' whose posterior they kiss and in whose form Satan appears to them' (p.174). In his book *The Edge of Evil*, Jerry Johnston states that 'The Cathars were perhaps the first group to actively worship Satan. Cathar traditions include belief in the equality of Satan and God, encouragement to choose Lucifer or Satan as the god to be worshipped, and the development of satanic ritual from the reverse of Christian liturgy' (p.153). Developing this theme, Carl Raschke – who is promoted as 'America's leading authority on Satanism and contemporary occultism' and who, as a Professor of Religious Studies at the University of Denver, ought to know better – claims that the 'so-called Black Mass' 'evolved from Cathar ritual', and that 'in the twelfth and thirteenth centuries there thrived offshoots of the Cathari calling themselves 'Luciferians'. The Luciferians were noted for such disgusting rituals as kissing a toad or the buttocks of a priest, not to mention the veneration of a black cat' (*Painted Black*, pp.88 and 89). Elsewhere in the same work he speaks of 'the old Catharism dressed as Satanism' in connection with the Nazis.

What is most disturbing about this is the subtle linking of nonsense about heresies of the past with nonsensical accounts of esoteric movements of the present. There are no Cathars alive today to suffer from persecution engendered by libel, but Theosophists are at risk when they, too, are presented as virtually satanic by such as Mrs Cumbey (see p.20 above). Nor is hostility to the Theosophical Society confined to America, it is also found in England.

For Michael Cole, Madame Blavatsky was 'greatly influenced by demonic spirits,' and he refers to 'The Plan' she was given 'for the ordering of the world in the last days, and for the coming into the world of the Antichrist' (*What is the New Age?*, pp.97–8). No reference to primary sources is given to support these claims, and one's confidence in Mr Cole declines still further when he founds the Theosophical Movement in 1844 (as opposed to 1875 in reality) and claims that after Madame Blavatsky's death, 'the Theosophical Movement was led by a lady called Annie Besant, who became better known as Alice Ann Bailey' (p.98). Kevin Logan (*Paganism and the Occult*, p.110) does not conflate these two formidable women; he merely has Mrs Besant as 'an outrageous accomplice' of Alice Bailey, but he does insist that *Isis Unveiled* and *The Secret Doctrine* were 'both produced in a trance state and automatically written under the guidance of the "Masters."' All that these fantastic fictions achieve for the informed reader is to arouse both wonder and despair at the depths of fundamentalist ignorance.

Another topic on which such writers are prone to error is the kabbalah – the traditional mysticism of Judaism. Their folly ranges from seeing Jewish mysticism as the 'esoteric and occultic book *The Kabala*' (Martin, *The New Age Cult*, p.15) to describing it as 'borrowed from Aramean Chaldeans in Babylonia' and being 'influential in the rise of the Knights Templar' (Paul Sturgess, writing anonymously in Perry (ed.), *Deliverance*, p.57), and presenting it as an amoral system: 'In the Kabbalah, good and evil are transcended in a great and etheric knowledge of the divine Oneness.' (Raschke, *Painted Black*, p.107). Every one of these statements is false.

Nor is the ignorance confined to historical and biographical

facts. The very nature of the New Age and everything associated with it is misunderstood and misrepresented. When
writing on the topic, even the most educated of fundamentalist
critics seem to throw reason to the winds. Thus the Reverend
Kevin Logan (in *Paganism and the Occult*) while professing
to avoid 'the use of emotive language which might prove
insensitive and offensive to those on the fringe of the occult'
(p.10), proceeds to lambast the New Age. Among a plethora
of hostile comments he sets out a New Age 'creed' that includes
such choice statements as these: 'The first commandment is
to love your self with all your mind, with all your heart and
with all your strength'; and '[the New Ager] is called to the
realization that he is part of the [universal] force, the force is
god, and therefore he is god' (pp.106–107). The setting-up of
straw men to demolish is an old trick of disputation, but one
would yet hope for supportive evidence.

One might expect as much from the American writer, Walter
Martin, a widely read and respected fundamentalist Christian
critic of cults in general. But when he approaches the New Age
his critical faculty dissolves into diatribe. *No* New Age cultist,
he maintains, can be a true Christian; indeed must oppose
Christianity: 'The New Age Cult's attack upon the person of
Jesus Christ – and attack is surely what it is – concentrates
on Christ's unique claim to deity.' (*The New Age Cult*, p.38).
Later, a paranoid tone enters in: 'The New Age political
agenda is dangerous because it is based on a monistic and
pantheistic world view. As such, the New Age political agenda
is anti-theistic and anti-Christian' (p. 69). Other writers take
this theme much further, but even this one comment helps to
sow the seeds of prejudice and animosity.

The New Age is by its nature a nebulous concept, and this
very nebulosity is made to serve its opponents' ends:

> Although the New Age does not have all the usual mani-
> festations of a movement – no central organization, no
> headquarters, no hierarchy, no creed – yet it is an unholy
> alliance throughout the world challenging the rule and
> authority of God. (Cole *et al.*, *What is the New Age?* p.107.)

That the same author earlier states categorically, 'The New
Age consistently teaches that a personal god does not exist' –

and thus, presumably, cannot be challenged – is an inconsistency that his readers are presumably willing to overlook.

Whether or not such statements are the product of wilful ignorance, there is a general lack of intellectual rigour in the work of the fundamentalist when contesting those things he abhors. Indeed, this is one of the principal weaknesses of such writing. By avoiding precision and seeking to pack all of 'the occult' within the limits of the New Age, the fundamentalist becomes at once all-embracing and ineffectual.

This is illustrated clearly from the work of Roy Livesey, a former supporter of the Findhorn Community who is now a 'born again' Christian. In one of his many books on the subject, *More Understanding the New Age*, (pp.64–9), he lists 145 'areas of occult that can often provide the clue to New Age activity'. His bizarre lists – he gives another of eighty 'cults' and a third of 120 'Holistic Healing Therapies' – include such odd 'occult' bedfellows as Addictions, Stonehenge, Electric Shock treatment, and Indian Elephants; Roman Catholicism and Buddhism offered seriously as 'cults'; and Contemplative Prayer, Placebos, and Aversion Therapy presented as 'Holistic Therapies'. What is most disturbing about such lists is not the author's lack of discrimination, but their effect upon his trusting but ill-informed readers.

And also ill at ease, for the hysterical tone of such books by Livesey, Mrs Cumbey and others on what may be termed the 'conspiracy' wing of fundamentalism cannot be anything but harmful to those who are already anxious and disturbed. It is less likely to affect those who turn to fundamentalism as a bulwark against anxieties and fears stemming from social changes, economic ills – both personal and national – and political uncertainties. But then *all* fundamentalists fully believe that the New Age and all that is associated with it is anti-Christian, and while such convictions are derived principally from a partisan interpretation of specific biblical texts and from preaching based on such an interpretation, they are strengthened by reading books that offer an appearance of scholarly support for their stance.

There is also a strictly limited and clearly defined market for such books: they are designed by the converted for the converted, and it ought to be the case that so long as they are restricted to such circles there is little or no risk of the myths and fantasies they contain being propagated among the general public. But investigative journalists and other writers are now turning to the 'occult' and the New Age as a fruitful field for the exercise of their talents, and when they build – as they often do – on a foundation of total ignorance, insatiable curiosity and a high degree of credulity, their initial research inevitably leads them to close encounters with spurious material of the kind quoted above.

Because of their own lack of expertise in the field, they tend to treat such works as authoritative, with the dire consequence that the most bizarre fantasies are repeated, with the truth still further embroidered, to the public at large. Current examples of books of this nature are Andrew Boyd's *Blasphemous Rumours*, and Tim Tate's *Children for the Devil*. Neither author is a fundamentalist, but we shall encounter both of their books again.

There are other avenues, too, by which fundamentalist perceptions of the New Age reach a wider audience. Michael Cole's book *What is the New Age?* contains many of the outrageous statements about its subject-matter that one expects from fundamentalist authors; but the book is issued by a major publishing house, Hodder & Stoughton, which effectively guarantees that it will have a far wider distribution than would be the case for a book issuing from a more inward-looking fundamentalist press.

Newspapers, too, propagate 'occult' follies derived from such dubious sources (for example 'Why the Occult still keeps us spellbound' in the *Daily Mail*, 9 August 1989), and their distribution is vastly greater than that of printed books. Even more insidious is misinformation spread through the medium of television. Specific programmes concerning allegations of Satanism are dealt with elsewhere, but individual documentaries are necessarily less influential than the regularly broadcast shows of the 'Televangelists'.

So far Britain has been largely free of television broadcasts devoted to evangelical religion (although independent radio evangelism is a growing phenomenon), but in America televangelism is firmly entrenched. There is considerable dispute as to its influence in terms of conversions or public acceptance of the socio-political attitudes of the televangelists, and even as to audience size. But what is not in dispute is that audiences for religious programmes in America are measured in millions. A Gallup survey, reported in 1987, indicated that seventy million Americans (thirty-two per cent of the population) watched a religious programme at least once a month, and while this was not confined to evangelical or fundamentalist programmes, it does indicate an enormous potential audience.

Other research has produced conflicting results, giving audience figures of between nine and forty million viewers for televangelist programmes. In his book *Pray-TV*, Steve Bruce concludes that there is a weekly audience of some fifteen million viewers for such programmes, that is, approximately eight per cent of the total viewing population. This would suggest a limited influence, but these are the committed viewers, already inclined towards fundamentalism. When the New Age is castigated by televangelists – as it frequently is – the distortions and sheer fictions broadcast are taken in by casual viewers also, to reinforce, and be reinforced by, similar misconceptions drawn from other sources.

Thus not only fundamentalists, but many in the general population are fed with false and negative beliefs about the New Age and alternative beliefs in general. They may not be consciously memorized, but they are recognized whenever they are re-presented, and arguments that present them in pejorative terms more readily receive general assent. The implications for potential persecution are clear.

Informed students of these subjects are well aware of the nonsensical nature of much that passes for 'research' in the mass media and popular books, and they are able to counter it with historical truth. What are more difficult to rebut are the sensational stories emanating from ex-Freemasons, ex-witches and ex-Satanists; it is even more difficult to gauge the effect on public opinion of supposed 'revelations' in the form of the personal memoirs of these various converts to fundamentalist Christianity. A large part of the content of their 'memoirs' is derived not from reality but from popular works on 'the occult' and from the overt fiction of Dennis Wheatley and other novelists whose work includes themes of magic, witchcraft and Satanism. Underlying this veneer of fantasy are the inner experiences of deeply disturbed persons which pose a problem for the critic. How does one counter these sensational claims, which have not the slightest basis in reality yet have a dangerously negative effect on public tolerance of alternative beliefs, without further harming the already damaged psyches of their authors?

There is no simple answer to this problem, and I can suggest only a refusal to mirror the aggressive approach of these 'converts' and their manipulators, while firmly refusing to countenance even the least of their fictions. Given the frustration of those who have suffered as a consequence of these personal memoirs, this is a counsel of perfection. But reacting in kind serves only to reinforce and widen existing prejudice.

What manner of story is put about by these people? It is usually a tale rich in sex and violence, and designed to show the absolute wickedness of all things 'occult'. Such tales also have a long and dishonourable history. During the first half of the nineteenth century they had much the same content as now but with different actors; then the principal hate object of fundamentalists was the Church of Rome, and the stories – in the form of the memoirs of escaped nuns – were of rape, torture and murder by monks and priests.[1]

One of the first of the modern wave of 'revelations' was Doreen Irvine's autobiography, *From Witchcraft to Christ* (1973). In this she claimed to have been introduced during the early 1960s to 'the most ancient order of Satanism in the world' in a two-hour ceremony involving 'about five hundred people' culminating in the sacrifice of a white cockerel. At her eventual initiation, at which 'about eight hundred or more Satanists were present', she drank blood, made vows to Satan and signed a parchment in blood 'thereby selling my soul to Satan for ever and ever, to be his slave for all eternity.' Following this, 'the people went crazy, and all kinds of evil scenes followed. Much wickedness was done that evening.' (p.94)

Her allegations are not even original since similar scenes were shown in the film version of '*The Devil Rides Out*', which appeared in 1968, five years before her book. There is an uncanny similarity between her description of a satanic ceremony and incidents in that film.

Miss Irvine went on to become 'Queen of the Black Witches' after performing remarkable 'supernatural feats' at a secret meeting of 'over a thousand witches' on Dartmoor – a curious meeting given that she describes the principal difference between Satanists and Black Witches as being that 'witches attend a coven of thirteen witches. 'They are every bit as bad as Satanists', for 'very often they exhume fresh graves and offer the bodies in sacrifice to Satan. They break into churches, burn Bibles and prayer books' (p.97). Worse than this, 'all meetings included awful scenes of perverted sexual acts, as sex plays an important part in witchcraft. Many black witches were lesbians or homosexuals' (p.98). In this way the association of perversion and occultism was implanted in the minds of her credulous fundamentalist readers. As we shall see, this association was to re-emerge some fifteen years later with devastating results.

In a later work, '*Spiritual Warfare*', she describes satanic temples (complete with statues of Satan, a gigantic altar and huge flaming torches) as being hidden inside ordinary-looking large houses – despite the presence of four hundred or more people engaged in orgiastic devil-worship. It is difficult to see how such an event could go unnoticed by the neighbours – unless, as was more probably the case, it never happened.

This analysis may satisfy the unbiased reader, but it is rejected by fundamentalist readers who continue to quote her work (which is still in print) and to treat her story as true. That her conversion to Christianity helped to alleviate her psycho-spiritual distress cannot be denied, but her relief has been obtained at the expense of truth.

Other converts to Christianity have offered lurid accounts of their suffering at demonic hands as a consequence of their involvement with Freemasonry. One, David Vaughan, describes in his book, *The Diary of a Freed Mason* (1990), how he encountered in his home, in broad daylight, 'a massive "heap" of impenetrable blackness possibly eight feet tall and nearly three feet wide.' This 'Darkness' dispersed when he managed to utter the Lord's Prayer, and he suddenly realized what he had faced: '"Darkness Visible" – the meaning for me was now quite evident, it is Satan. The Masonic Ritual [in which the expression occurs] now appeared in quite a different light, sinister, threatening.' But a careful reading of Mr Vaughan's text reveals the psychological pressure he was experiencing at the time and indicates the purely subjective nature of his experience. By projecting the negative images of his own subconscious mind on to Freemasonry, he undoubtedly hastened his own recovery, but at the expense of unjustly smearing an honourable institution.

The certainties of fundamentalism provide a safe haven for those under stress, but the fantasies, errors and misconceptions that they bring with them are taken up as realities and thus help to sustain fundamentalist prejudices. Nor is the New Age and all that is associated with it the only object of those prejudices and the hostility that goes with them. Even the Church is not immune from fundamentalist attack.

NOTE TO CHAPTER TWO

1. Examples are the mythical Maria Monk; and Rebecca Reed, whose 'experiences were related in sensational and often reprinted popular 'autobiographies'.

THREE

Unlikely Allies

The majority of fundamentalists hold their beliefs from free choice, while a minority – whose exact size cannot readily be determined – seize upon dogmatic beliefs as an antidote to personal stresses and anxieties, or as a refuge from social and political uncertainities. Both categories of believer will maintain a hostile attitude towards any faith or practice that conflicts with their own certainties, but it is an attitude determined by faith rather than by expediency. There is also a third category, consisting of individuals whose fundamentalist faith is indisputable but whose attitude towards other belief systems – even those within mainstream Christianity – is determined by more complex motives.

These are the managers of the faithful, the ministers, pastors and priests, whose lives are committed to propagating a dogmatic, simplistic faith and ensuring doctrinal purity among their flocks. Unlike the members of their congregations they must continue to maintain a high public profile; they cannot fade into inactivity if faith becomes lukewarm, nor even let the fire of their faith fade in the slightest degree. If that were to happen then the very meaning of their lives would be lost. And it is they who are in the vanguard of the true faith, preaching by the spoken and the written word, and campaigning in the war against spiritual evil, whether it manifests itself openly as some aspect of the New Age, or more subtly in the dilution of faith that accompanies liberal theology.

In some respects this perceived corruption within the

Church is seen as more dangerous, and fundamentalist clergy are active in opposing it – often to the detriment of the Church itself. Their approach is exemplified in the work of the Reverend Tony Higton, the Anglican Rector of Hawkwell in Essex, who in 1984 founded 'Action for Biblical Witness to Our Nation' (ABWON). This organization is vehemently opposed to critical questioning of Christian doctrine and to anything within the Church that can be construed as unbiblical. Its hostility is directed in equal proportion to the alleged idolatry at Walsingham (where Anglican and Roman Catholic processions and services honour the shrine of the Virgin Mary); to multi-faith festivals and services (such as the Canterbury Festival of Faith and the Environment in 1989, against which Mr Higton actively campaigned); or to any sign of tolerance towards homosexuals – Mr Higton has referred to the *Church Times* as 'a vehicle for homosexual propaganda' simply because it proposed Christian forbearance (letter to *Church Times*, 23 February 1990).

Most recently Mr Higton's energies have been directed especially towards opposition to multi-faith services. In December 1990 he delivered to Buckingham Palace a petition with 76,965 signatures, urging the Queen to ban multi-faith Commonwealth Day services from Westminster Abbey and to ensure that they are made explicitly Christian. The Queen rejected the petition and attended the service (on 11 March 1991), but Mr Higton remained undaunted.

Soon after his royal rebuff Mr Higton set out, in the *Church Times* (22 March 1991), the purpose of the petition:

> Our problem with the Commonwealth Day Observance is that it effectively puts Jesus on a level with other deities or figures like the Buddha. It puts all religions and all scriptures on a level. It marginalizes Jesus and encourages worship of other deities. . . . it will confirm people of other faiths in their opinion that Jesus is merely a prophet. And that will be a further disincentive for them to consider the truth of Christ as the incarnate Son of God and of his atoning death.

In September 1991 he was instrumental in the circulation among Anglican clergy and influential laity of the 'Open Letter to the Leadership of the Church of England' which set out the anxieties of its signatories with regard to multi-faith services. While acknowledging the 'rights and freedoms' of those of other faiths, the letter expresses concern that the 'Gospel shall be clearly presented in this Decade of Evangelism.' It expresses deep concern about 'gatherings for interfaith worship and prayer involving Christian people . . . [which] conflict with the Christian duty to proclaim the Gospel. They imply that salvation is offered by God not only through Jesus Christ but by other means, and thus deny his uniqueness and finality as the only Saviour.'

There is, of course, nothing wrong about devout Christians expressing their concerns, but the letter goes on to appeal to 'the leadership of the Church of England to oppose and, where possible, prevent such gatherings for interfaith worship and prayer in the Church of England and to seek to discourage them elsewhere.' It further points out that the signatories' objections are not only theological and spiritual, but also constitutional. Such words and sentiments suggest the intention of taking legal action to stop multi-faith worship. Thus does embattled exclusivity turn to active intolerance.

And the letter did not fall on stony ground. By December it had received two thousand signatures. At the same time a poll of clergy, conducted by the *Church of England Newspaper* while the 'Open Letter' was circulating, found that more than half were opposed to inter-faith services. Most disturbing was the fact that among the signatories were the principals and senior staff from five theological colleges, suggesting that future ordinands would be increasingly narrow in their outlook.

This is borne out by the attitudes implicit in a letter to the *Church Times* (24 April 1987) from twenty-nine students at Chichester Theological College, who expressed their 'horror' at Southwark Cathedral receiving a donation from Freemasons. They went on to state that Freemasonry is 'a perversion of the Christian gospel' and 'a dangerous distortion of our faith.' And this irrational and wholly unjust condemnation comes from men who will go on to influence the faithful of many parishes during their working lives.

Nor does such a blinkered attitude stop at letter-writing. When the Reverend Bob Simmonds wrote of his distress at seeing his 'local church torn apart by a group of Evangelical Charismatics who, having caused pain and division in the church, have left to form their own "house church"' (*Church Times*, 14 June 1991), it elicited a response that encapsulates the self-righteousness of the Charismatic. The Reverend Brian Favell (Letter, *Church Times*, 21 June 1991) commented that he was 'very aware of the pain – even oppression – suffered over a long time by both lay people and clergy who have discovered the living Lord and Holy Spirit, yet find their experience ignored, their theology rubbished and their hunger unfed by so many of their pastors and peers.'

Implicit in this letter is the suggestion that the faith of non-Charismatics is in some way inferior. It contrasts starkly with this timely warning in Mr Simmond's letter:

> My anxiety is that, as a Church, we seem to be moving towards an uncritical attitude towards, and over-dominance by, the more fundamentalist, Evangelical and Charismatic end of our tradition, at the expense of the open, liberal, critical, pastoral and intellectual positions that have been some of our strengths in the past.

In justice to these fundamentalist clergy, however, it must be stressed that their vocations are not in doubt and that there is no question of financial gain being a hidden motive for their behaviour. The same cannot be said of all purveyors of fundamentalism.

More than ten years ago sales of evangelical religious books and records in the USA reached a total of nearly $1,000,000,000 – more than a quarter of gross sales of the entire commercial book market at the time.[1] Their sales have not declined: one of the most popular of apocalyptic fundamentalist works, Hal Lindsey's *Late Great Planet Earth*, has sold eighteen million copies. The financial stakes in the marketing of fundamentalism are clearly high.

Even this would not be worthy of special comment were it not for the fact that many of the more successful authors are perhaps less than discriminating when recommending dubious books by some of their colleagues. These successful authors – whose endorsements virtually guarantee sales – enthuse over books filled with fantasies, errors and misconceptions.

The authors of fundamentalist diatribes may become wealthy from their work, but there is nothing to suggest impropriety in their dealings – which cannot be said for some of the televangelists. Fund-raising has always been an important element of religious broadcasting in America, and a fair proportion of donations is generally put towards such worthwhile charitable projects as schools and hospitals. The techniques of persuasion directed at the viewer may sometimes be tasteless – as with Oral Roberts, who in 1986 claimed that God would call him home unless $9 million was raised for his medical school; it was raised, and Mr Roberts did not die – but the money is usually directed at the cause concerned.

American fundamentalists expect their ministers to live well and the televangelists do their best to oblige. Given the level of income, a glamorous lifestyle is not difficult to achieve: in 1979 an analysis of televangelism gave annual figures of $50 million for Jim Bakker's *PTL* (*Praise the Lord*) *Club*; $46 million for Jerry Falwell's *Old Time Gospel Hour*; and $31 million for Jimmy Swaggert: (J. A. Haught, 'Gospel Millions' in the *Charleston Gazette*, 9 September 1979 and subsequent issues). It was further noted by Mr Haught that religious revivalists found 'universities' because as university presidents 'they can pay themselves large sums of money without IRS [Internal Revenue Service] scrutiny.' As preachers they cannot do this.

Of course, not all televangelists are dishonest. But there is one spectacular exception. In 1987 Jim Bakker gave up control of PTL following revelations of his sexual misconduct. This alone might have been forgiven in time, but allegations have been made of financial impropriety on a large scale, involving expensive and luxurious homes for Bakker and his wife; an outrageously lavish lifestyle; and blatant nepotism involving his brothers.[2] For some, greed is evidently a major motivating factor in their promotion of fundamentalism.

All of these examples, whether the individuals concerned are honest or not, indicate the wealth, power and influence that are at risk if popular fundamentalist support is lost. To retain that support requires that the numerical strength of fundamentalism be maintained, and this in turn requires that existing fundamentalists hold on to the beliefs and fears that keep them within their peer group. One of the most powerful ingredients in the mortar that binds together fundamentalist bodies is fear and loathing of all beliefs and activities that can be attributed to Satan. Thus for the fundamentalist minister or manipulator who is motivated by the desire for personal success, propagating the ignorance which perpetuates that fear and loathing is an essential activity.

There may also be the need to maintain power structures; especially within hierarchical institutions such as the Roman Catholic Church. Since the election of Pope John-Paul II, the relative liberalization of the Church following the Second Vatican Council has been reversed. In part this has been a response to the decline in numbers of both laity (see p.16 above), and clergy – more than 100,000 priests gave up their ministries in the years following Vatican II, and numbers of ordinands are in serious decline. It is also a reaction to both liberal and 'liberation' theology, which stresses the importance of the 'social gospel'. This reaction has come at a time when the Charismatic Movement is growing within the Roman Catholic Church, and there is increasing official concern about, and hostility to, all perceived manifestations of the New Age – Catholic studies of which are now as credulous and ill-informed as those of Protestant fundamentalists.[3]

Catholic hostility towards, and distorted image of, such institutions as Freemasonry mirrors that of Protestant fundamentalism, but despite the shared attitudes and beliefs of the Charismatic Movement that is now growing within both, there is virtually no co-operation between the two traditions in their approaches to their perceived common 'enemies'. As yet there have been no mutual attacks mounted upon the New Age. But away from spiritual warfare, in the field of social campaigning, doctrinal differences have been set aside in order to fight against the evil effects of 'secular humanism' – especially those stemming from the general relaxation of strict codes of sexual morality.

The most prominent and visible result of this has been the action of conservative Catholics uniting with Protestant fundamentalists in the crusade against abortion. Both groups perceive the increasing rate of abortions in Western countries as the most pernicious effect of the 'secular humanist' assault upon the traditional family unit, and their vehement and often violent opposition to legalized abortion has brought religious fundamentalism firmly into the political sphere. Although organized anti-abortion campaigns began in the USA, as a reaction to Supreme Court decisions that liberalized laws relating to abortion, they have taken deep root in Britain and Ireland – to the extent of copying the illegal activities of the militant American anti-abortion group, Operation Rescue. The nature and implications of those activities will be considered elsewhere in this book.

But while the rise of single-issue campaigning organizations has brought together disparate strands of religious fundamentalism, it has diluted the strength of more broadly based movements within the New Christian Right. The principal casualty has been Jerry Falwell's Moral Majority Inc. which was closed down by its founder in August 1989.

For the ten years of its existence Moral Majority had provided a link between fundamentalism and politics that enabled religious conservatives to become right-wing political activists. By 1989, however, both its membership and its annual income – which had fallen from a peak of $11.1 million in 1984 to only $3 million – were in serious decline. But it had served its purpose. Its success in bringing fundamentalists, who traditionally turned their backs on national politics, into the political arena led *The Wall Street Journal* to describe Moral Majority as 'one of the major forces propelling America to the right' – a shift that 'helped make abortion an evil word to many, school textbooks a censorship matter and racy advertising a reason for boycott.' (R. G. Niebuhr, 'Spent Crusade' in *The Wall Street Journal*, 25 September 1989).

Falwell himself has since turned his energies to promoting his Liberty University at Lynchburg, Virginia, into an institution that will help to entrench fundamentalist ideas in the mainstream of American culture. In twenty years it has seen a spectacular growth: from a handful of students to a roll of over 8,000. But the newly awakened political awareness of fundamentalists does not readily translate into an influence on the major issues of national and international politics; it is more concerned with purely social issues, and does not wish to be drawn into the wider political world. The attitude expressed by Tom Minnery, vice-president of the Focus on the

Family organization, is typical: 'Moral Majority took stands on South Africa. Man, we don't do that !' he said in the above quoted article from *The Wall Street Journal*. 'Our organization is concerned with the health of the nuclear family.'

The intrusion of fundamentalist beliefs and prejudices into the political world is not confined to the USA and is not confined to committed believers. In Britain it has surfaced both nationally and locally as politicians manipulate fears that are grounded in the distortions of fact propagated by fundamentalist ignorance. Political attacks upon Freemasonry, for example, play upon allegations of financial, legal and political corruption that are made in books principally concerned with its supposed anti-Christian nature.

This has resulted in a bizarre, symbiotic relationship between conservative fundamentalists and largely agnostic politicians and activists of extreme left-wing leanings. It is unlikely that there is any overt, conscious co-operation between individuals on either side, but the errors and innuendoes in the claims of the latter have their origin in the hysterical denunciations published by the former.

As an illustration of the process a relatively recent *cause célèbre* in Bristol, involving an alleged masonic element, is exemplary. A training scheme for the jobless in south Bristol, the Knowle West Employment Venture, collapsed with enormous debts and under suspicious circumstances – to the extent that a police investigation was carried out. Three prominent critics of the scheme, including Vernon Hicks, a left-wing Labour member of the City Council, subsequently suffered from a bizarre and unpleasant hate campaign in the course of which abusive telephone calls were made, referring to a 'Mr Lodge', a 'Mr Mason' and a 'Mr Tyler'. From these names – with their possible masonic overtones – Mr Hicks deduced that masonic corruption was involved in the scheme and that he and his colleagues were being attacked by unidentified Freemasons. Despite there being not one shred of evidence to link either the Employment Venture or the subsequent hate campaign with Freemasonry, Mr Hicks remains adamant that Freemasons are involved. Subsequently a radical local journal, *Venue*, published a feature article ('Conspiracy of Hate', 4 December 1987) which, while professing to be impartial, was blatantly anti-masonic and further fuelled the cause of intolerance.

As a consequence of this affair Labour members of Bristol City Council demanded that masonic membership be declared by all councillors and council employees. To date this potential witch-hunt has not taken place, but demands for it have resurfaced. In October 1990 Terry Walker, a Labour member of Avon Council, claimed that candidates for jobs in the police force and fire brigade had attempted to suborn him with 'Masonic signs' – but to no effect because, in his own words; 'As a Socialist, I am violently opposed to Freemasonry . . . they seek to further the interests of their own members.' Other Labour councillors backed his views and argued for a voluntary register 'so council officers could declare membership of secret societies.' These councillors are entitled to hold such views, but that discrimination on grounds of personal belief and social activity can be seriously proposed gives cause for alarm.

More recently the suggestion that Freemasons interfere with the course of justice has been made in dramatic fashion. Shortly after the successful culmination of his campaign for the release of the wrongly imprisoned 'Birmingham Six', Chris Mullin (the Labour MP for Sunderland South) said – in the course of a speech on miscarriages of justice, delivered at a meeting of the Legal Action Group – that he 'could not be certain whether masonry had contributed to the wrongful imprisonment of the Guildford Four, the Maguires and the Birmingham Six, but that a public declaration of membership would eliminate doubt.' He went on to say: 'We can at least then see where everyone is coming from. It is a serious problem in both the legal profession and the police.' (*The Observer*, 23 March 1991.)

Other British politicians, more directly involved with fundamentalists, have voiced even more outlandish opinions. One of them, Geoffrey Dickens, Conservative MP for Littleborough and Saddleworth, has campaigned vigorously against what he identifies as paganism and the occult. For some years he has sought to persuade Parliament to legislate against the occult, most recently in February 1991. But while he makes extravagant claims in the House of Commons he refuses rational debate with his opponents. On 15 April 1988 he said: 'It is common knowledge in this House that many people who have been charged with and convicted of offences against children were involved in witchcraft initiation ceremonies. We need a chance to discuss the workings of witchcraft and how it can be controlled in this country.' 'Common knowledge' has long been a convenient excuse for offering no evidence, and Mr Dickens has yet to offer support for his view in any public forum outside the privilege of Parliament, even though he has proposed an amendment to the Criminal Justice Bill that would render it illegal for persons under the age of eighteen years to 'join, participate in or be present at any secret occult ceremonies or groups.'

His views are redolent of those expressed by the former Conservative MEP for Avon, Richard Cottrell, who in June 1982 began an investigation into the activities of the Unification Church (popularly known as the 'Moonies') which he soon extended to include other cults and sects alleged to be harmful to young people and to break up families. Mr Cottrell was inspired to mount, and to extend, his investigation because of the 'weight of evidence reaching him', much of it as a result of a lobbying campaign by parents of cult members, carefully orchestrated by a network of fundamentalist anti-cult groups. He was not the first politician to view the new religious movements with alarm. In August 1981 the Labour MEP for Glasgow, Janey Buchan, and the Socialist MEP for Frankfurt, Mrs Weiczorek-Zuel, had called on the German Parliament to refuse residence rights to three hundred Moonies. Their desire to restrict the activities of this cult stemmed from the laudable motive of seeking to protect the young and vulnerable, but they had undoubtedly been stimulated by fundamentalist propagandists.

There had also been a sustained media campaign against the cults, notably in the *Daily Mail*, which also tended to reflect fundamentalist beliefs and all the errors of fact that went with them. The anti-cult campaign has subsided, but it has been replaced with an almost obsessive media interest in the question of Satanism. Whether or not there really *are* any Satanists is not an issue that is addressed; but the alleged effects of Satanism, child abuse and human sacrifice, are analysed in depth.

In general, British newspapers do not peddle a fundamentalist line, but the tabloid newspapers tend to be more credulous when reporting 'occult' activity, and to be more willing to print the views of fundamentalists even if they do not espouse them in editorials. As a consequence, a large section of the British public remains remarkably ill-informed about the New Age and alternative beliefs in general. This ignorance is compounded by supposedly 'investigative' television programmes that are heavily biased towards credulity (for example, the two Channel 4 *Despatches* programmes on Satanism, and *The Cook Report* of July 1989 on the same subject).

It must be admitted, however, that most serious newspapers in Britain take a relatively objective line over the issue of alleged Satanism and maintain an honourable and praiseworthy stance over the question of religious freedom. But they often display a marked hostility towards alternative therapies and psychic practices, using the weapon of derision against the latter, whether or not the specific case deserves serious analysis.

This is exemplified by their treatment of the highly controversial psychic, Uri Geller. A feature on him in *The Independent on Sunday* of 30 November 1991 ('Fighting Psychic', by Amanda Mitchison) treated him in a condescending manner and was biased in favour of the views of Geller's arch-opponent, James Randi. The general tone of the article was also clearly hostile to all things psychic. It may well be that Geller does not have any psychic ability at all, but he is entitled to ordinary courtesy, and even if psychic phenomena ultimately prove to be chimaerical, they still merit objective examination. The unthinking sneers of the sceptic help to promote an atmosphere of intolerance just as much as do the credulous fears of the fundamentalist.

Newspapers are also not immune to the bandwagon effect. When one takes up a sensational subject and prints alarming reports about it the others follow. The way the subject is treated necessarily depends on the cultural composition of the readership: what may be believed and approved of by readers of the *Sun* or the *Daily Mirror*, may be greeted with indifference by those of the *Daily Mail* and may prove intolerable to readers of *The Independent*. But in the absence of accurate and objective information there is a probability that all uninformed readers will believe what is presented to them.

When the topic in question concerns unorthodox religious belief, the supernatural or the New Age, the prevailing lack of reliable information readily available to the public ensures that fiction will outweigh fact and that speculation will take the place of certainty. The continuing lack of reliable source material also prevents journalists from producing accurate reports, articles or reviews and ensures the perpetuation of ignorance. And if those who are competent to assess what is published complain, and demonstrate the falsity of wild accusations and sensational claims, their complaints are relegated to the letter pages. Equally, those who have been maligned obtain little redress unless libel is involved; the nominal 'right to reply' of the aggrieved usually results in a tiny paragraph on an inside page. Newspaper editors do not like to admit that they may occasionally be wrong.

On occasion, however, they may make the *amende honorable* – albeit in a somewhat oblique manner. Thus *The Mail on Sunday* was instrumental in exposing the fantasies of Michelle Smith, which gave birth to the wave of hysterical 'satanic child abuse' stories that swept across America and Britain in the 1980s, although in the early part of the decade its sister newspaper, the *Daily Mail*, had been at the forefront of similar scaremongering stories about the evils of the 'cults'. But in general there are all too few signs of an active campaign by the media to increase the general level of religious tolerance; opposition to the *fatwah* pronounced against Salman Rushdie is muted by deference to shrill cries of 'blasphemy' from the self-appointed zealots of Muslim fundamentalism who are quite unrepresentative of their own community. There is all too little acceptance of what ought to be axiomatic in a pluralist society: intolerance is itself intolerable.

Nor are intolerance and persecution the stock-in-trade of fundamentalists alone. Politicians may mount or support popular crusades against perceived spiritual wickedness, but this is as often a matter of expediency – to counter fading local or national popularity, or to act for pressure-groups within a parliamentary constituency – as of conviction. There is also the intolerance of the scientific establishment, less noticeable to the general public but no less damaging in its effect upon individuals who dissent from scientific orthodoxy.

The motives for scientific intolerance and active persecution are quite clear. There are the personal fears of losing status and of jeopardizing academic careers consequent upon the propagation and acceptance of views that undermine the dogmatic beliefs of the established scientific world-view. This suppression of dissident views within the scientific community is more than a simple reversal of the situation in early-modern Europe, in which the Church repressed scientific theories that conflicted with its own interpretation of the universe because they threatened its mechanisms of control. There is also a personal element: the wish to maintain existing views of the laws of nature when these underpin personal faith; when radical reinterpretations of the structure of matter and the nature of life are proposed they not only threaten the status quo of accepted scientific theory but also disturb the equilibrium of the individual psyche.

But when opinions are dogmatically stated that can be utilized by fundamentalists in attacks upon alternative therapies (for example), they are eagerly taken up and used as ammunition – even when the implications of the opinions so used may be equally damaging to the fundamentalist world-view itself. Fundamentalists and scientific researchers may make uneasy bed-fellows, and the bases of their attacks may be radically different, but to the object of such attacks they can be equally damaging.

Thus 'scientific' opposition to homoeopathy (the therapy which seeks to alleviate the symptoms of disease by administering infinitesmally small doses of substances that in larger quantities will induce similar symptoms) is based on the assumption that dilution to the extent involved (typically to 1 part in 10) can leave no trace whatever of the substance concerned. That there may be some unrecognized or unidentified physical process involved in the action of homoeopathic remedies is categorically denied – cures are put down to a placebo effect. How this accounts for the success of homoeopathic remedies in preventing mastitis in cows is not explained, but the reason for the hostility is clear: if homoeopathic remedies are more effective than allopathic ones in a variety of circumstances, then there is less scope for employment in the drug industry, which is itself thereby threatened.

Fundamentalist critics of homoeopathy are, in one sense, less blinkered than the chemists whose data they use. While denying a 'scientific' basis to homoeopathy, they recognize the inadequacy of the placebo effect as an explanation of the cures it effects. In its place they claim that success comes from 'the activity of spiritual forces whose intentions are not as benign as that of some of the homoeopaths.' And because the research that led him to discover this system of therapy had no scientific basis, Samuel Hahnemann, who pioneered it, was necessarily 'deceived by a lying demonic spirit' (A.D. Bambridge, *Homoeopathy Investigated*, c. 1989, pp. 3 and 7).

Other areas of mutual concern to fundamentalists and the scientific establishment are the fields of psychic phenomena and astrology. The latter topic has been responsible for two of the more disgraceful of modern episodes of scientific intolerance. The first was the determined attempt to suppress *Worlds in Collision*, a book published in 1950 by a Russian psychoanalyst, Immanuel Velikovsky, who put forward a series of bizarre, and ultimately untenable, theories about the solar system. Instead of ignoring Velikovsky's work, a number of distinguished scientists, led by the astronomer Bart Bok, mounted a campaign against it. The publishers of the book, Macmillan & Co., were threatened with a boycott of their entire list by a large number of American universities and colleges if the book remained on sale. Faced with this virtual blackmail, Macmillans gave in and *Worlds in Collision* was withdrawn.

Happily freedom of expression found other champions and the book was soon re-issued. Velikovsky's opponents moved on to other targets. In 1975 Professor Bok was instrumental in issuing *Objections to Astrology: A Statement by 192 Leading Scientists* to the effect that 'there is no scientific foundation for its tenets' and 'no verified scientific basis' for the continuing faith of those who believe in astrology. The reasons they offer for their concern are interesting.

They were 'especially disturbed by the continued uncritical dissemination' of astrology by the media and by 'otherwise reputable newspapers, magazines, and book publishers', which 'can only contribute to the growth of irrationalism and obscurantism.' It is this that makes it necessary for them to 'debunk beliefs based on magic and superstition.' Finally they state: 'We believe that the time has come to challenge directly and forcefully the pretentious claims of astrological charlatans.'

Six years after the publication of this 'Statement', Dr Robert Morey issued his pamphlet *Horoscopes and the Christian*. With the addition of a charming conviction that 'astrology has always been, and still is, a branch of black witchcraft', Dr Morey's approach is much like that of the humanist scientists. Astrology for him is 'lacking in any validity' and 'its only appeal to modern man is by way of superstition and magic.' They attack astrologers as charlatans; he attacks them as occultists (which, for humanists, is virtually synonymous with charlatans). Neither thinks of tolerating astrology, although astrologers attack neither empirical science nor Christianity, but Dr Morey is more cautious in rejecting any scientific defence of the subject.

The principal proponent of objective statistical study into the claims made by astrology is Michel Gauquelin (he does not claim that his own research *proves* astrology), but his work is derided by Professor Bok and his colleagues. Dr Morey is more cautious and admits that the validity of Gauquelin's research is still undecided. In this he provides a rare example of fundamentalist tolerance outdoing that of supposedly objective humanist scientists. But are they objective?

They are certainly not always discriminating. Professor Bok's co-author, Laurence Jerome, demonstrates his own credulity when he cites two books of doubtful value – William Seabrook's *Witchcraft: Its Power in the World Today* (1941), and D.H. Rawcliffe's *Psychology of the Occult* (1952) – to demonstrate that the psychological effects of magic can produce death. This is on a par with fundamentalist warnings of its demonic nature and gives little confidence that the objectors to astrology are wholly objective.

That they are not is demonstrated by the behaviour of members of CSICOP (Committee for the Scientific Investigation of the Paranormal) in 1982 when faced with further evidence that Gauquelin's findings (on the predominance of specific planets in the horoscopes of members of different professions) were statistically viable. Since that time Gauquelin's work has been endorsed by the psychologist Hans Eysenck, but because these findings went against the preconceptions of the CSICOP investigators, they prevented their publication in the Committee's journal, *The Skeptical Enquirer*. This was scarcely consonant with scientific investigation and led to CSICOP's founder, the sociologist, Professor Marcello Truzzi, quitting the Committee in disgust.

Scientific intolerance within CSICOP has been demonstrated more recently with its refusal to accept evidence from Italian studies that tend to support the theory underlying homoeopathy. And yet CSICOP receives regular media praise for its 'honesty' in unmasking psychic fraud.

In this its prime activist is the Canadian stage magician James Randi who, though not a scientist, is treated as an ultimate authority on psychic investigation. During July and August of 1991 Mr Randi presented a six-part series on British television, entitled *James Randi: Psychic Investigator*. Subsequent media reports indicated that he had demolished the assorted mediums, astrologers and other psychics who had faced him, but in practice he had not. He trumpeted his successes – which were duly recorded by the press – and brushed aside his failures: he was, for instance, unable to fault the dowser, Michael Cook.

At least one reporter, Lynne Truss in *The Times* of 20 July 1991, noted that his series was curiously mistitled. An 'investigator' implies someone who does field studies and approaches the subject with a genuinely open mind. In Randi's case he baited his subjects, who were working in far from ideal test conditions, and treated the whole affair as what it was in reality: popular entertainment before a studio audience. It is less than honest for CSICOP to proclaim victory over the supernatural when it determines the rules and proceeds to act as judge and jury.

All of this may seem somewhat laboured, but it is essential to realize that nominally objective empirical scientists, committed to the search for truth in nature, are not always paragons of virtue in the matter of upholding the right of freedom of belief. Fundamentalism is not the only source of intolerance and subsequent persecution; on occasion the religious fundamentalist finds an unexpected ally in the empirical scientist – albeit an ally who will not hesitate to turn on fundamentalism itself when the opportunity arises. The belief system of the atheist and the agnostic is as rigid and as narrow as that of the biblical fundamentalist, and as with all such 'closed mind' systems it will seek to suppress whatever threatens to shake its foundations, whether it be a rival belief system or an unwelcome scientific discovery.

NOTES TO CHAPTER THREE

1. *Charleston Gazette*, 10 September 1979. Based on sales of $600 million by the 2,800 members of the Christian Booksellers' Association, plus the comparable sales of the 35 per cent of non-member retailers.
2. Full details are given in Bruce, *Pray TV*, chapter 10.
3. Examples are LeBar, J. J., *Cults, Sects, and the New Age*, Huntington, Ind., 1989; and Brennan, J., *The Kingdom of Darkness*, Lafayette, La., 1989.

FOUR

Battering Belief

One significant difference between scientific and fundamentalist hostility to astrology, psychic phenomena and all other unorthodox beliefs and practices, is that the former is based on a denial of the validity of such beliefs and of the reality underlying them, while the latter accepts the reality but imputes it to an evil source. It may make little difference to the embattled astrologer or spiritualist whether he is battered with a sceptical club or a religious brickbat, but the manner in which the attack is conducted and justified depends very much on the direction from which it comes.

The scientist may on occasion use specious arguments and underhand means, but his is a relatively ineffectual assault as far as the general public is concerned, and it rarely leads to actual persecution. (It is a moot point as to whether Mr Randi's pursuit of Uri Geller constitutes persecution; Geller thinks that it does and the matter is currently being determined in the courts.) We need not consider this further and may thus turn to the way in which fundamentalists set about their campaigns, looking first to their words before we examine their deeds.

Astrology is neither the most frequent nor most significant target of fundamentalist wrath, but of all such targets it is the one most widely recognized – and believed in – by the general population of both Britain and the USA. The majority of people treat daily newspaper horoscopes with little respect; some may believe in them but most readers look upon them as harmless fun. Not so the fundamentalist. For him it is the first step on a slippery, downward slope which involves a broad spectrum of practices that all have only one end. This downward journey is graphically described by the Reverend Steve Morgan of Merthyr Tydfil:

> Devil worship and satanic ritual involving human sacrifice and the sexual abuse of children is the end of the road in a downward spiral of moral depravity.
>
> That journey can begin ... with nothing more than an interest in horoscopes or simple superstitions, and lead to dabbling with ouija boards or tarot cards – both of which are advertised in newspapers and magazines, and legally available across the counter at occult centres throughout Britain.
>
> The next stage may involve an interest in Spiritualism, and even attempting to become a medium.
>
> People of like mind, meeting through advertisements in the Press or in the back room of video shops selling illegal hard-core pornography, form themselves into secret covens in which they can worship Satan. (The *Western Mail*, 14 August 1989.)

His comments were designed for public consumption – and a large public at that; the *Western Mail*, in which they appeared, has the largest circulation in south Wales – and if his readers were troubled that was no more than what was intended. To the fundamentalist evangelism is of prime importance; he does not seek simply to warn an indifferent public against the wickedness of all things occult, but reasons that if they can be drawn away from them then they are more likely to turn towards his own form of belief, and to the hope of salvation that it offers. It is thus important that the futility and wickedness of such things are made plain.

In the process factual accuracy and the reasoned debate that ensures it may well be neglected, as with the Reverend Kevin Logan, who condemns astrology because 'the biggest problem with astrology is that it stops people from worshipping the one true God. They are too busy worshipping balls of dead matter wandering through space.' (*Paganism and the Occult*, p.124.) One need not believe in astrology to know that this is a nonsensical statement – Mr Logan had probably read Morey's *Horoscopes and the Christian*, in which the following comment is made in order to show that astrology is polytheistic: 'The stars are viewed as deities who have the will and power to determine man's destiny' – but it reflects the uncritical thinking of even educated fundamentalist Christians.

Similar nonsense is disseminated about the other practices that the Reverend Steve Morgan finds so dangerous. Ouija boards were originally designed as a means of recording supposed messages from the spirit world; today they are marketed as a board game. The board has the letters of the alphabet, numbers from 1 to 9 and, occasionally, other symbols printed around the edges. Messages are built up by recording the sequence of letters and numbers indicated by a pointer, mounted on castors and moved – supposedly unconsciously – by the fingers of the participants in the game. An inverted tumbler is frequently used in place of the mounted pointer. The ouija board has been especially singled out for condemnation by fundamentalists, being seen as a source of psychiatric disturbance and worse. A particularly dramatic warning against them is given by Mrs Maureen Davies, a founder of the Reachout Trust, a body whose principal purpose is to combat both 'the occult' and cults in general. (This Trust plays a significant role in fundamentalist intolerance in Britain; its stated aims and objects are printed in Appendix 1.) In an audio tape distributed by the Reachout Trust (*How to Deal with the Occult in Your Area* 1989) Mrs Davies states that 'we have friends whose friends committed suicide through playing with ouija boards. We have got letters from parents whose children are in psychiatric hospitals and have been 'sectioned' because of ouija boards.' One would expect evidence to be offered for such startling claims, but she gives no names, no locations and no dates. Nonetheless, the seed is sown and Mrs Davies's hearers will go in mortal terror of a foolish board game.

In fairness to fundamentalists it should be noted that they do occasionally offer rational justifications for their fears. Thus Kevin Logan (*Paganism and the Occult*, p.130) quotes the comments of a colleague, John Allan, 'an experienced Christian in the field of parapsychology and the deliverance ministry.' Speaking of the ouija board, Mr Allan said:

It is possible to bypass the censor which normally filters the impulses deriving from our subconscious, and let things out which ought to be kept in. In fact I think there is overwhelming evidence to show that at least some of the time a ouija board can be a device (like a crystal ball or a pendulum) for releasing the forces of the subconscious in an irresponsible way, which can cause untold damage to the human personality.

Whether or not the evidence *is* 'overwhelming', is a moot point. More typical is a remark by Peter Anderson in his book *Satan's Snare*:

People treat the ouija board as a game, but it has proved to be dangerous and destructive. 'Ouija' is the combination of the word 'yes' in both French and German. The devil always says 'yes' to his followers. They do not like 'no' for an answer, therefore they shall have 'yes'. (p.21)

Spiritualism itself, which institutionalizes that communication with the dead which was the original purpose of the ouija board, is also on the road to Hell. For the fundamentalist it is not the spirits of the dead who communicate:

There are only two sources from which spirits come. One is from Satan or the devil, these are known as evil spirits or demons. The other source is from God, these are known as angels or messengers. The question is, of course, where do the spirits that are invoked in spiritualism come from? (Diasozo Trust, *Spiritualism, a Dangerous Counterfeit, c.*1989)

As spiritualism is equated with necromancy (divination through the spirits of the dead, called to the necromancer by magical rituals) it comes as no surprise that the source is Satan. The pamphlet quoted above goes on to spell out just what these spirits do:

The desire for communication with the spirits of the dead can lead to terrible disaster. Every aspect of your life can be cruelly affected by evil spirits looking for nothing better than an opportunity to destroy, [because by so doing] they hope to keep people from the reality of God and cause them to enter into eternal torment.

The methods employed by the demons are choice: 'Spiritualists and their children are ravaged by mental disorders and
nervous problems.' If this were so there would be grounds
for real alarm, but not the slightest piece of evidence to
substantiate this is put forward. When individual cases of
mental illness are cited to justify condemning spiritualism
they invariably lead one to the conclusion that the mental
disturbance preceded and led to the involvement with any
psychic activity rather than the reverse.

But even without evidence to support their case, fundamentalists are convinced that they are right, citing biblical authority in the many letters they write to the national
and local press, condemning such activity. A letter to the
Bristol Evening Post (9 February 1990) decrying the Bristol
Psychic Fair, will serve as an example: 'These practices are
an abomination to God, who forbids people to indulge in
them.' Another Psychic Fair followed in 1991, drawing a
forthright condemnation from the Reverend Maldwyn Jones
of the pentecostalist New Life Christian Centre in Bristol.
Where it differed from the previous year's protest was in
gaining prominent media coverage. Mr Jones was quoted at
length.

He urged people to stay away from the event, because it was
'an open invitation to evil', and affirmed his belief that 'all occult
practices, including palmistry and clairvoyance, come from the
same source – which is satanic.' He went on to say that, 'the
Bible clearly states that all forms of astrology and the occult
are witchcraft and sorcery and should be avoided. The whole
thing is a very sinister business and should not be treated in a
jocular fashion. It is at odds with Christian teaching.' (*Western
Daily Press*, 6 April 1991.)

The newspaper also gave the opposing views of those taking
part in the fair, but the headline was hostile: 'Churchman
hits at "evil" psychic fair.' Similar negative press coverage
was given later in the year to a projected course in 'psychic
awareness' at a Bristol library. The report, by Judith Skorupski
in the *Bristol Observer*, 2 August 1991, gave equal space to
the two opposing views, but the headline – 'Pastor's Fury
at Devil in Library – and opening paragraphs, referring to
'evening classes run by two occult worshippers', went to the

fundamentalists. Paul Jackson, the minister of a pentecostal church at Knowle in Bristol, said that the classes 'could be damaging, especially to young people. They can get sucked deeper and deeper into the occult, until they are driven out of their minds.'

Once again there is the emphasis on the threat to innocent and vulnerable youth, an emphasis that is found in a large proportion of fundamentalist assaults upon alternative beliefs and practices. It is not something that occurs by accident; it is perceived as an ideal way in which to arouse public alarm. And such alarm is not allayed by sensational headlines and the one-sided prominence of press reports. However, spiritualism is well enough organized to fight back, and disputations in newspaper letter columns do not always end in fundamentalist victory. When Eric Clarke, of Christian Information Outreach, was quoted in the Bristol Journal (4 December 1986) as saying 'the spiritualists are being deceived by demon spirits who are impersonating the dead', he received more (and better informed) opposition from spiritualists than support from fundamentalists.

The scaremongering by fundamentalists, for such it is even though the sincerity of their beliefs is not in doubt, is not confined to seances and psychic fairs. Even children's books can be doorways to evil. One month before Christmas 1991 – at just the right time to affect sales – fundamentalists in California brought a court action against a local school authority for allowing into schools books which 'incite devil worship'. The books in question were not popular horror stories of the Stephen King variety, but classics by J.R.R. Tolkien and C.S. Lewis, the worst offender being Lewis's *The Lion, the Witch and the Wardrobe*. How a book which is a thinly disguised parable of the crucifixion and resurrection of Christ can promote Satanism was not explained.

Spiritual healing is also looked at askance unless it takes place in the context of fundamentalist – usually Charismatic – worship. Thus the healer Agnes Sanford is condemned by the evangelist Peter Anderson, as 'one of the instigators of the "New Age" deception (*Satan's Snare*, p 65) This gentle spiritual healer would seem an unlikely source of evil – her approach influenced many Christian Charismatic healers –

but Anderson's lack of charity is such that he finds her philosophy variously 'blatantly spiritistic' and 'pantheism done up in a Christian garb'. In his eyes her greatest evil was in looking upon the Bible as only one source of inspiration among many. And for him this should 'warn us quite clearly of the pit from which her teaching comes' (p.67). Elsewhere in the same book he quotes the comment by the ex-medium Raphael Gasson to the effect that, 'There are many spiritualists today, who are endowed with a remarkable gift of healing by the power of Satan' (p.20).

Other problems connected with spiritualism were identified among a group of rather more orthodox healers (nurses), by David Lewis, one of the authors of the book *What is the New Age?* He reported a statistical analysis of a survey of 108 nurses that he conducted in 1986, from which he found that 'it is clear that an involvement in spiritualism is associated with reduced levels of psychological well-being, lower levels of expressed "happiness", and less generous attitudes towards others' (p.114). But his sample was far too small for the results to have any significance for nurses as a whole, let alone the general population. But this alleged depressant effect of spiritualism pales into insignificance when compared with the alarming statement tacked on to the end of Mr Lewis's study:

> In modern Britain there are many people who have become involved to a lesser or greater extent with activities of this nature [i.e. ouija boards, and consulting fortune-tellers]. There are also some who are involved in the worship of Satan, 'black magic' and witch covens; among some of these groups it appears that child sacrifice is currently being practised. (p.116)

Yet again the specious link is made between spiritualism and Satanism.

Satan rears his head with even greater frequency in fundamentalist comments on Hallowe'en. In his book *The Occult – Deliverance from Evil*, the Reverend Russ Parker condemns Hallowe'en practices:

> Much damage is done by Christians who mix up Christianity with the occult by encouraging this practice, which

is pagan at heart. For too many children this annual pre-occupation with evil leads to a deepening fascination with the supernatural, witches, and the possibility of exercising power over others. (p.33)

He cites no evidence whatsoever to justify this claim, but he does reproduce with approval a leaflet entitled *Hallowe'en*, issued by the Association of Christian Teachers.

According to Parker (p.33), the leaflet was issued 'in response to this popularization of something that is intrinsically evil.' He quotes the following justification:

1. If we suppose that witches and spirits are nonsense, why, then, encourage children to celebrate their mythical frolics and perhaps take them seriously? Paganism is hardly a cultural mainstay of all that is best in our society.

2. Suppose that in our folklore, witches and demons merely represent moral evil. Hallowe'en then tends to celebrate evil in the ascendant by the reversal of moral standards. If Nazi figures were regularly presented for children's admiration and affection there would soon be a public outcry. But lovable little witches are brought out every autumn. This disturbs the polarization of good and bad, right and wrong, in children's minds.

3. Hallowe'en does in fact encourage an interest and fascination in the occult and this invariably leads to more serious involvement and damage to the individuals concerned.

No evidence is given to back any of these assertions, but such statements have led to deliberate interference with children's education. For example, in October 1988 an evangelical Christian group at Rydale in North Yorkshire successfully called for a ban on any celebration of Hallowe'en in local schools; while in Clwyd, north Wales, the standing advisory committee on religious education 'asked schools in the county not to celebrate the festival or make an issue of it in the curriculum' (*Western Mail*, 12 October 1990). This was backed by a petition (with 120 signatures) 'expressing concern at the way the festival was celebrated in schools' and it was expected that the request would be heeded. The justification given was that 'there were now fears among all denominations that it could foster a dangerous fascination with the occult among the young.' Once again, no evidence was given to support these fears.

Even more alarming is the deliberate – and wholly unwarranted – association of Hallowe'en with Satanism made in 1989, by Mrs Maureen Davies, in the course of her lecture on her 'American Trip'. Mrs Davies claimed that:

> At present we've got five crises leading up to Hallowe'en where children are being, are going to be ritually abused or sacrificed, and we have to link in and work with the police departments in saving these children. At present we have had three enquiries where we've been tipped off where children are going to be sacrificed or be in the sex rituals. We have been able to involve the police, and the police have prevented these from occurring. (Transcript, p.37)

Mrs Davies will figure again when the whole question of supposititious 'Satanism' is considered. Here it is enough to point out that no police department has any link with her and that on no occasion have the police reported the rescue of children from potential sacrifice.

But it does bring up again the prominence of the alleged threat to children. For fundamentalists the nuclear family is the basic and ideal social unit, a paradigm for society in general, and hierarchically structured in accordance with their understanding of biblical injunctions on relationships within the family. Any perceived threat to the stability and continuance of the nuclear family is thus seen as something to be fought against, and the suggestion that children might be alienated from their families by involvement in the 'occult' arouses as much alarm as any threat to their spiritual well-being. This is not to suggest that fundamentalist parents are not concerned for the physical and mental welfare of their children. As with all parents, the image of children at risk evokes in them a powerful emotional response which is exploited to the full in fundamentalist propaganda.

It is manifested particularly in two fields: in cult membership and in Satanism. Children are posited not only as both innocent and vulnerable, but also as essentially honest and reliable witnesses to what they may have experienced. The suggestion that statements by small children – especially those concerning matters in which childhood fantasy may play a role – should be treated with caution, or that they are themselves suggestible in the course of questioning, is firmly rejected. In its place we are urged to listen to the children; to believe the children. This emotive appeal has helped fundamentalists to gain popular support among the general public – especially for anti-cult campaigns and for efforts to promote the myth of Satanism. For the most part, fundamentalists cannot be accused of cynicism in this manipulation of children; they truly believe that supernatural evil is rampant in the world, and they are often not conscious that what they do causes any harm. But harmful it is, and when we come to consider what fundamentalists have done in pursuit of their goals we shall see what appalling miscarriages of justice can result from their actions. We shall discover also how elastic is their definition of the term 'child'.

The strict definition of a cult has been given in Chapter 1 (p.21), but it is as well to consider that for the fundamentalist the term has only a pejorative meaning – thus the more appropriate term of New Religious Movements is rarely used in fundamentalist circles. Many cults are unquestionably destructive in the effect that they can, and often do, have upon their members, but the simplistic view that *all* cults are undesirable and wicked is both inaccurate and dangerous. The effects of cult membership set out in the Cultists Anonymous pamphlet (*see* Appendix, 2) do not necessarily follow: there are many balanced and articulate members of such 'cults' as Scientology and the Unification Church, who live fulfilling lives in the wider community. Similarly, not every factor listed in the table 'Mark of Cults' in the same pamphlet applies solely to destructive cults; at least one of them – 'Members are preoccupied with fund-raising, recruiting and worship exercises' – could be applied with equal justice to many well-established Christian denominations.

It is as well also to take note of the description of a cult given by a delegate to the 11th Annual Virginia Crime Prevention Conference, at Chesapeake, Virginia, in June 1989. The speaker was Robert Hicks, a criminal justice analyst with the law-enforcement section of the Department of Criminal Justice Services in Richmond, Virginia, and a man well qualified to assess the legality or illegality of any given cult:

> I wish to alert you, to a dangerous cult that has implanted itself not only in Virginia but throughout the country. This group, called the Tnevnoc Cult, is a 'communal, sectarian group affiliated with a large and powerful international religious organization.' I can communicate something to you of the methods and goals of the organization by describing the cult's recruitment and indoctrination practices.
>
> The cult aims to recruit young women, either teenagers or young adults, and does so openly at schools and colleges. Following indoctrination into the cult, young women eventually lose any power of will, succumbing entirely to the regimen of the cult.
>
> Cult members must abandon their former lives, even surrendering their outside friendships and personal possessions. Cult members' activities then involve the cult exclusively. Members must rise at 4.30 in the morning, wear prayer beads attached to their wrists, engage in long monotonous chants and prayers, and in one of the most bizarre activities, members consumed food they were told represented the dead cult founder's body.
>
> Women must even pledge in writing absolute obedience to the cult. To further distance itself from worldly affairs, the cult assigns new names to members and designates as their birthdays the dates of their entry into the cult.
>
> After hours of performing menial tasks such as scrubbing floors coupled with incessant recitation of ritualistic prayers, members might occasionally transgress rules which are punished harshly. For example, punishment might require women to go without food, having to beg on the knees for crumbs from others' plates.
>
> But the most shocking ritual of all required members to become brides to the dead cult leader.
>
> I hope that I have sufficiently aroused your curiosity, if not your indignation and anger, that such activities could happen in the United States. In case you haven't figured it out, Tnevnoc is Convent spelled backwards. I have just

described the socialization of young women into Christian convents. (R. Hicks, *Satanic Cults – A Sceptical View of the Law Enforcement Approach*, N. Hollywood, Ca., 1989)

Mr Hicks might have specified that the details he gave applied specifically to Roman Catholic convents and that their regulations have been greatly liberalized since the reforms of Vatican II. But his account serves to emphasize that first appearances are not always sufficient for a final judgement of any given cult, sect or church.

Here I must again emphasize that I do not advocate the doctrines or practices of any cult or sect. All of them should be judged by their obedience to the law of the land and their conformity to the prevailing moral code. However unorthodox the beliefs, however bizarre the practices, if these do not stray outside the law, then any cult has an absolute right to go about its business in peace, unhindered by those who may disapprove of its tenets. But if it exerts undue, illegal pressure on its members, if it encourages them to break the law, or if it mistreats them and so breaks the law, then its leaders must face the rigour of the law.

In practice, however, few cults engage in illegal activities. The majority of cult members join as adults by free choice. This may cause alarm and hurt to their families, but if persuasion does not succeed in changing the adult cult-member's mind, there is no justification for using forcible means to extract him or her from the cult in question. The real illegality arises when cult-members are kidnapped on behalf of their families; they are held against their will; and they are subjected to 'deprogramming' techniques. And the inspiration for such activity has often come from fundamentalist sources.

Among the most active of these has been the Deo Gloria Trust, based at Bromley in Kent, whose chairman, Kenneth Frampton, has for many years been prominent in national and international bodies dedicated to exposing the wickedness of the cults. The success of Deo Gloria in spreading its message in the early 1980s was largely due to Caryl Matrisciana, a journalist who, as Caryl Williams, was Press and Publicity Officer of the Trust. Mrs Matrisciana also had charge of Deo Gloria Outreach, the evangelical arm of the Trust, and was responsible for the dissemination of information about the cults to the public, and thus for moulding the fundamentalist image of cults in general: an image that is all too easily fed back into the public mind by way of subsequent books and press reports.

The Deo Gloria Trust, however, utilized more modern propaganda techniques. In 1985 Caryl Matrisciana and her husband, Pat, produced the highly successful anti-cult films *Gods of the New Age* and *Cult Explosion*. The publicity material for the latter identified many of the more destructive cults – as perceived by fundamentalists:

> Untold millions today are in spiritual bondage to the Cults or occult. The film *Cult Explosion* is a searing exposé on the insidious anti-Christ working of groups throughout America. Former leaders of many cult groups explain the secret inner core of such groups as: Peoples Temple; Worldwide Church of God; Moonies; Hare Krishna; Christian Science; Scientology; Mormons; Jehovah's Witnesses; TM; Black Muslims; Unity; and the Manson Family . . . and how they found freedom and eternal life in the real Jesus. If Christians are to deal with the dramatic increase in the cults in our nation today . . . they must see *Cult Explosion*.

The Matriscianas also worked closely with another prominent fundamentalist, the author Dave Hunt, whose book, *Peace, Prosperity and the Coming Holocaust* was the source for much of the material in *Cult Explosion*. The book is virulently hostile to Hinduism, which is presented not only as the source of the majority of cult beliefs, but also as actively inimical to Christianity. The potential threat to children is also introduced: 'In schools across the Western world, from kindergarten to universities, Hindu occultism is being openly taught in spite of otherwise enforced separation of church and state.'

Throughout the film version of *Gods of the New Age* (and in her book of the same name) Caryl Matrisciana presents an extremely prejudiced view of Hinduism, which is given an unwarranted authority because she was born and raised in India. Thus she says, 'I have personally talked with many, many gurus and the sad fact is that with their belief system they have to be detached and removed from their emotions and compassions and their cruelty and inhumaneness is seen as spiritual and excused as holy.'

Elsewhere in the film, a Danish cult expert, Dr Johannes Aagaard, states that at the heart of the cults is 'the guru concept, the sense within Hinduism, the personal dimension.' Having reinforced the link between the cults and a supposed anti-Christian Hinduism, Mrs Matrisciana continues with her hostile views, again stressing the threat to children and to the traditional view of family relationships:

> In some schools of thought, to be spiritual celibacy is encouraged and yet in others sexual perversion is practiced, not only among the gurus themselves but by their disciples including young children. Contradictions are also seen in the attitude towards women who, on the spiritual level are the purpose of worship, their femaleness is seen as the creative power of God. For instance to be initiated by a female yogini is considered much holier than initiation by a male. And yet on a day to day level women are considered lower than men and treated as less than human.

The threat of the cults to children is reiterated by another cult expert, the German Pastor, Friedrich Haack:

> Children brought up in a cult are only educated to follow the commands of the leaders. They never experience freedom, they never experience a responsible life where they could have their own choice, where they could follow their will.

And with the link between cults and Hinduism firmly cemented, a final doom-laden warning is given:

> The religion that is out to destroy Christianity is being embraced by millions, including many in the Church today, who are naively succumbing to spiritual propaganda and unwittingly becoming disciples of the gods of the New Age.

The other great exponent of cult wickedness is Maureen Davies, but she is also an activist. In her taped lecture, *How to Deal with the Occult in Your area,* Mrs Davies stated that she and her fellow 'Christians' had 'picketed every T[ranscendental] M[editation] meeting in our area [Rhyl, North Wales]' for

three years, interrupting and disrupting the meetings until
'we haven't had a TM meeting this year [1989] at all.' TM
also fares badly at other hands. In his pamphlet *Transcendental
Meditation is Dangerous* (1982), Mike Taylor of the Charismatic
Diasozo Trust, states that 'TM opens people up to demonic
manifestations, such as so-called "Extra-Sensory Perception"
and "Psychokinesis".'

He is, of course, entitled to voice such an opinion, but it is
dangerously misleading to make such erroneous comments as:
'A mantra is a magical spell or prayer to a demonic being under
the disguise of a Hindu god,' and 'TM involves the worship of
the deceased guru Brahmananda Sarasvati.' Too much anti-
cult material depends on overt hostility to the Hindu religion.

But cults are not the only organizations to be assailed by
fundamentalists. There exists a modern Order of Druids,
that professes the gentle philosophical beliefs that the ancient
Druids are presumed to have held, although the modern Order
has no historical connection with them. For fundamentalists,
however, the Druids were wholly evil.

The outrageous John Todd, who held American fundamentalists enthralled in the 1970s with his manic tales of
Satanism, witchcraft and conspiracy in high places, claims
to have been a Grand Druid Priest, and to know the truth of
their activities. In *Spellbound*, one of the 'Christian' comics of
the fundamentalist publisher, Jack Chick, Todd alleged that
the Druids sacrificed young women at Hallowe'en (thus laying
a trail of fictions that would end with the school bans described
above), and that Stonehenge was 'the temple site for many of
these occult murders.'

Whether or not he believed this nonsense, the outspoken
English evangelical, the Reverend Tony Higton, attacked
modern Druids by innuendo when he inveighed against the
use of Saint James's church in Piccadilly for non-Christian
lectures and meetings. 'Earlier in the year [1989] the Chief of
the Druid Order lectured on Druidism. The ancient Druids
were the religious representatives of the Celts, who worshipped
a horned fertility god. Sometimes this god had as consort the
"Earth Mother". Celtic Religion included human sacrifice.'
(*What is the New Age?* p.51).

It is not simply the Druids whom Mr Higton is attacking. He

objects strongly to the work of the Reverend Donald Reeves, who is the incumbent of Saint James's. Mr Reeves seeks to minister to New Agers and as a part of this 'Alternatives Ministry' he holds a variety of 'New Age' lectures, workshops and other events in his church. In Higton's words this is 'a New Age programme which has links with the occult' and 'the fact that this is allowed in an Anglican church is, of course, a scandal of the first order', due to 'the spineless "tolerance" of much Anglicanism [that] not only leaves the door open to New Age infiltration; [but also] puts out the welcome mat'. (*What is the New Age?* pp.49 and 52.) It should also be noted that similar attacks upon activities at Saint James's are made by Maureen Davies in her lecture cited above.

Neither of these activists sees fit to refer to the 'Friendly Disclaimer' printed on the 'Alternatives' programme. This clearly states that: 'Although Saint James's Church, in its generosity and openness of mind, hosts Alternatives, the ideas in the Alternatives programme are not representative of Saint James's Church itself.'

Many will disagree with Mr Higton's views, but what is disturbing about his diatribe is that the book in which it appears was suggested by David Wavre, an editor at Hodder & Stoughton (who published it), after hearing tapes of a conference for Church leaders 'to consider New Age teaching'. If major publishers – whom one assumes to be both cultured and sophisticated – uncritically accept that the 'New Age' is about 'forbidden and unbiblical practices', then intolerance in word is upon us, and the danger of intolerance in deed – of persecution – is brought closer.

Tolerance itself is unacceptable to fundamentalists when it concerns religious belief. Ecumenism in any form is wholly unacceptable – fundamentalist churches do not affiliate to the World Council of Churches and, as we have seen, all too many evangelical Christians reject utterly the idea of inter-faith gatherings. The consequences of this hostility are expressed succinctly in a comment on the Anglican "Open Letter" in *Omega News*, (No. 46, Winter/Spring 1992): 'The aggressive certainties of the 'open letter' will do no more than close off yet another option for growth and mutual understanding, the one form of common witness which our sadly irreligious age so desperately needs.'

The Omega Order itself, which is based at Winford, near Bristol, attempts to provide that common witness. It is 'an ecumenical religious community for men and women. The Order exists to practise and to enable others to develop the disciplines of contemplative prayer and meditation, and to explore the evolution of spirituality.' But to the fundamentalist mind it is anathema, and so the Reverend John Bolton, who is the incumbent at Winford and a conservative evangelical, actively preaches against the work of the Order.

There is, however, no reason to suppose that the Order will not survive local intolerance. But in the wider Church the prospect is uncertain as long as such movements as ABWON (see p.48 above) flourish. Even their views pale besides those expressed by Roy Livesey. For him the Roman Catholic Church is 'a counterfeit Christianity' that is 'poised also for ecumenical unity with New Agers, with ecology groups and the occultists, also with the rest of Satan's religious deceptions'. (*More Understanding the New Age*, p.134.) Not content with this, Livesey goes on to condemn the Pope as Antichrist.

In his attitudes he is matched and surpassed by Jack Chick, of Chino, California, who for more than fifteen years has been publishing and distributing magazines (more strictly pictorial comic-books) designed to persuade their readers that anything which can remotely be considered 'occult' is Satanic and a threat to the human soul. While this may seem merely childish, there is a more pernicious side to such evangelizing of the semi-literate. Not only are the dubious claims of John Todd perpetuated (see pp.99 and 17) but the bizarre fantasies of an ex-Jesuit priest, one Alberto Rivera, are promoted as truth – encouraging readers to believe that the Roman Catholic Church is demonic, that the Popes are Satanists and that:

> Satan uses the Vatican to orchestrate our destruction. Very few realize that Rome is secretly united with the Illuminati, Masonry, Communism, Zionism and their subsidiaries to control banking and world commerce. They also use the media to manipulate almost everyone on Earth. (Alberto Rivera, *Double Cross*, 1981. p.29)

Further, the Church of today – especially the Jesuit Order

– is accused of torture, murder, treachery, espionage, war-mongering and every other imaginable crime, while every atrocity of the past is laid at the Pope's door. And this in addition to controlling Nazism, Communism and Islam; orchestrating both World Wars and master-minding the holocaust.

Rivera is, of course, careful to avoid libelling any living Roman Catholic (with the exception of the present Pope) but the specious assertions pedalled by him would appear to be designed to engender hatred between Christians of different denominations – and given the cultural limitations of the target readership of these comics he is likely to succeed in his aim. Nor are these comics confined to the USA. Over a three-year period, some half a million of these comics have been distributed in Britain by The Penfold Book and Bible House of Bicester in Oxfordshire, whose president, Michael Penfold, has stated that 'from what I've researched into the Roman Catholic Church I agree with what we've distributed, what it says doctrinally and historically' (*The Independent*, 11 March 1989). Nor is the Roman Church the only target of the Chick comics: Islam, together will all non-Christian religions, is attacked, as is the theory of evolution – in the last instance incorporating stereotypes of both Jews and 'New Agers'.

Rivera and Chick are not alone in their baseless attacks upon the Roman Catholic Church – they are also mounted by the ubiquitous Constance Cumbey. All of these, despite the wide distribution of their views, could be dismissed as of little consequence, but they act as a catalyst for hatred and intolerance not only within the Christian faith but also between different faiths.

Non-sectarian institutions fare no better. The innocuous Theosophical Society is a fount of all ills for some funda-mentalists. Perhaps the most wildly unjustified assault upon it is that by Constance Cumbey, who claimed that the Society freely acknowledged 'its demonic origins' and that it was (and is) characterized by 'theosophical hatred of Christianity'. She adds the nonsensical allegation that an 'order from these demonic messengers [the supposed Mahatmas] told them [the founders] to keep the Society and teachings secret – at least for the time being'. (*The Hidden Dangers of the Rainbow*,

Shreveport La., 1983, pp.45 and 46.) As this 'secrecy' was supposedly maintained until 1975 it is difficult to see just how the Society has managed to maintain its high public profile for the last century and more. Rational argument is not a fundamentalist strong point.

Rudolf Steiner, who broke away from the Theosophical Society, is also attacked. According to Michael Cole, the Waldorf Schools (which are based on Steiner's educational philosophy) 'began to indoctrinate the children' with 'strange ideas about Jesus', with the result that 'good schools with highly-trained and committed staff produced children who got a good education, but whose parents noticed their children degenerating spiritually. The parents, however, could not get to the roots of the fundamental philosophy. This is one more example of the deception and subtlety of the New Age.' (*What is the New Age?* pp.4 and 5.) These are serious allegations, but Mr Cole gives neither names, dates nor locations. But the mud will stick.

The greatest venom is reserved for institutions perceived as esoteric, or 'occult' Orders. Some of them, such as the Fraternity of the Inner Light, and its parent body, the Hermetic Order of the Golden Dawn, are just that, and while their activities may not merit the wrath of fundamentalists in the eyes of the world, one expects it. The same should not be true of Freemasonry.

Although it is a secular Order, with between five and six million members worldwide, Freemasonry is perceived by fundamentalists to be a religion. It exists to promote universal tolerance and social harmony, its basic principles being Brotherly Love, Relief (i.e. Charity in its broadest interpretation, as an active support of the community in every possible way), and Truth. And every Freemason must believe in God, although he does not have to accept any specific faith or denomination; indeed, there is not the slightest reason why he should, because Freemasonry is not in any sense a religion: it does not promote or advocate any specific religious doctrines or dogmas, and it does not engage in public or private acts of religious worship. Nor can there be said to be, in any sense, a 'Masonic God' as such; the individual Mason is required to believe in God, but it is for his own conscience to determine how he understands and worships God, and how he conceives both his personal and communal relationship with God. A body founded on tolerance would not and could not dictate to its members what religion they must follow; equally it neither could nor would accept among its members those who were dedicated to evil doing and to the worship of Evil personified. More succinctly, no Freemason can also be a Satanist.

But this is precisely what its fundamentalist detractors say Freemasonry is: Satanism. They have been saying it since the early eighteenth century, and the same distortion, error and deceit regularly recurs. Thus Edward Decker, an American Baptist minister from Washington State, can say:

> The Mason who would call himself Christian and allow himself to partake of a ritual resurrection by the power of Lucifer is no Christian. He is a Satanist. He stands, having been born again and raised from the dead as a Master Mason, through the power of the Masonic god, whom the God of Israel cast into the pit! (*Freemasonry not Compatible with Baptist Faith, c.* 1980)

Charismatic critics are no more gentle. Their attitudes are expressed in propaganda leaflets distributed by the Christian Publicity Organization (CPO) of Worthing (whose leaflet *Freemasonry* states that 'it throws a veil over the mind and can lead to real spiritual oppression'; and: 'If you are a Freemason, God wants you to agree with him that it is wrong'). A leaflet, *Can a Christian be a Freemason?*, issued by the Oxford New Testament Fellowship is littered with mistakes and wild misrepresentations: 'It has its own "temple", altar, hymns, prayers, chaplain, theology and god'. 'Inside it is a web of deceit'. Royal Arch Masons are accused of blasphemy and idol worship; the scurrilous assertion is made that 'A Freemason is under oath to favour other Freemasons' (which he is not); and far more disturbing is the insistence on renouncing Freemasonry and destroying everything personal connected with it.

More recently a bitter attack was launched in an allegedly 'carefully researched' book, *The Secret Teachings of the Masonic Lodge, A Christian Perspective*, by John Ankerberg and John Weldon (Chicago, 1990). This offers all the old canards but in a new package. Freemasonry is described variously as 'metaphysical Satanism'; 'a potentially occultic religion'; and as offering 'both an introduction to, and a furthering of, the cause of paganism, mysticism, the psychic and the occult.' A dispassionate analysis of Freemasonry shows no such tendency, and it can only be passed off as so by stretching the meanings of words to their limits after taking them from carefully selected quotations that represent only personal opinions.

In England the two most widely read books on Freemasonry of recent years, both bestsellers, are attacks on the Craft, but neither is the work of a Christian fundamentalist. Both books (*The Brotherhood* by Stephen Knight, 1983; and *Inside the Brotherhood* by Martin Short, 1989) are hostile tirades against the Craft. Both works rely on innuendo, unsubstantiated allegations, long-exploded canards and the testimony of deeply unreliable witnesses; but to the public their allegations and insinuations are simply 'facts'.

Stephen Knight quoted selectively from the papal Bull *Humanum Genus*, ignoring its attacks upon both democracy and secular education, and thus gave a false view of both its contents and context; he also made false allegations against named individuals that he was legally obliged to withdraw before the book was published, and other allegations that were removed before it was reprinted in 1985; but he then added without evidence or justification that Grand Lodge had banned 'Freemasons from owning, discussing or even reading the book.' His successor, Martin Short, produced a longer, more carefully written and altogether more malicious book – in that its innuendoes are more subtle, being cloaked in a skilful rhetoric which lends his allegations an easy plausibility.

Freemasons could, of course, ignore such attacks. But they are no longer the work of fundamentalists alone – although it is they who have continually stoked the fires of prejudice and ignorance – and false, damaging notions about Freemasonry are becoming common currency. If the attacks are not rebutted with vigour, then another group of unjustly maligned individuals will suffer from the smears of a noisy and bigoted minority.

FIVE

'Thou Shalt Not'

Many fundamentalists tend to be all-embracing in what they condemn and wish to forbid. For instance, Roy Livesey's absurd lists of 'areas of the occult', 'cults', and 'Holistic Healing Therapies' [*see* Appendix 3] include virtually everything that could remotely be associated with the general headings – together with much that clearly has no conceivable connection. He admits that not every entry 'need be necessarily occult', but all of them carry the risk. His reasons for producing the lists are not to encourage research, but to 'assist in recall of any past involvement and where identification and repentance is necessary', and also to allow the Holy Spirit 'to prompt a reminder, or to prompt further enquiry into what a son, or a daughter, or a friend, may be involved in that might not be right'. (*More Understanding the New Age*, p.64.) The possibilities for intrusion into privacy; for arousing needless feelings of guilt; and for the suffocating oppression of intellectual and spiritual freedom of choice are endless.

Surprising as it may seem, organizations devoted to global peace and harmony, and to preservation of natural resources, are not included in Mr Livesey's lists. But they are condemned by implication and he elsewhere makes full amends for any apparent omission. He remarks (*Understanding Deception*, p.21) that 'as a New Ager . . . I had been involved with the United Nations Association.' And this, by its central position in world affairs, is the very heart of the New Age threat.

For Mr Livesey the United Nations Organization is a part of

a satanic plan for world government: 'When we turn to the UN we are able to see for ourselves much of the diabolical evidence. The Meditation Room at the UN HQ in New York is shaped like a truncated pyramid (the Illuminati insignia) laid on its side' (p.23). This may seem quite lunatic, but although many fundamentalist Christians would not share his hostility to the United Nations, many others do and are led to reject a body that works for peace and reconciliation.

Nor are Mr Livesey's the only widely distributed books that promote this viewpoint. Others, too, see the UN as the most important of all New Age, and thus by implication, anti-Christian, organizations. Separatist fundamentalists, who studiously avoid involvement in politics because it links them with an apostate world, do not take part in campaigns against institutions – political or otherwise; but there are influential figures who do not share that viewpoint and who actively campaign against international political, economic and ecological co-operation.

Implicit in both Mr Livesey's writings and in that of Constance Cumbey, the Detroit attorney whose book *The Hidden Dangers of the Rainbow* is the most widely known and influential of all American anti-New Age works, is the notion of a satanic conspiracy to establish an anti-Christian 'New World Order'. Mrs Cumbey spells it out in alarming terms: 'for all practical purposes, the New Age movement appears to qualify as a revival of Nazism'. (*Hidden Dangers of the Rainbow* p.99.)

The diatribe that follows this statement begins with the patently false claim that: 'It is public knowledge that both Winston Churchill and Franklin Delano Roosevelt dabbled in the occult. Perhaps the same conspiring Luciferic spirit that induced Hitler to implement the darkest practices of occultism moved upon the Western powers to conceal the esoteric mysticism behind Nazism.' Worse follows: 'The New Agers have a slightly different order [than that of Hitler].' Jews are on the list as soon as they are finished with the Christians. But both groups are high on priority for persecution, with the Jews faring slightly worse than the Christians (pp.103–104). Mrs Cumbey then presents a detailed six-page 'correlation between Hitlerian Nazism and the New Age Movement', filled with gross errors of fact, and derived not from historical studies, but from the works of H.P. Blavatsky and Alice Bailey – both of whom are grossly misrepresented.

To his credit, Roy Livesey has more recently rejected many of Mrs. Cumbey's rantings, but he still insists on the underlying spiritual wickedness of all institutions dedicated to political unity or religious ecumenism: 'This global spiritual unity,' he says, '. . . results in the conscious worship of Lucifer.' Foolish this may be, but the works of both Livesey and his mentor are readily available in religious bookshops – and not only those of an evangelical cast – to misinform and to alarm the unwary.

Hostility to any form of co-operation between different faiths also leads Mr Livesey to attack the meeting of religious leaders at the 25th Anniversary meeting of the World Wildlife Fund at Assisi in 1986; and to condemn the 'Creation Harvest Festivals' held in Winchester Cathedral in 1987, and in Coventry Cathedral the following year. In particular he attacked HRH the Duke of Edinburgh, President of the World-wide Fund for Nature (then the World Wildlife Fund), for seeking to 'bring all the religions together.'

Prince Philip has also come under attack from other quarters, specifically over elements of the Duke of Edinburgh Award Scheme. Maureen Davies, of the Reachout Trust, referred to the scheme in one of her public lectures (Report on American Trip): 'Did you know that "Dungeons and Dragons" is part of the curriculum on the Duke of Edinburgh awards scheme ?' she asked her audience, and proceeded to tell them that 'Dungeons and Dragons' 'is really witchcraft or Satanism dressed up and called fantasy' and that it is 'actually just a way of promoting witchcraft.' This unwarranted slur on the Award Scheme is repeated in her lecture on *How to Deal with the Occult in your Area*, in which she refers to 'the dangers and the murders and the suicides which are now taking place because of Dungeons and Dragons.'

The image of Prince Philip as being in thrall to irrational gurus is also promoted by the press. He was reported – under a headline, 'Philip and guru stir unholy row' – as planning 'to undertake a pilgrimage to a sacred wilderness with a controversial spiritual mentor'. (*The Sunday Times*, 10 November 1991.) The announcement of this projected visit to Mount Athos in Greece led the Reverend Tony Higton to claim that the Prince had brought the Church of England and the Queen (who is its secular head) into disrepute because he had instigated the meeting at Assisi in 1986 that resulted in eight major religions proclaiming their commitment to protecting the environment.

An admirable cause was no excuse for what Mr Higton perceives as apostasy. He stated that 'Christians should not be involved in worship or prayer which marginalizes or even excludes Jesus Christ,' and added that 'this sort of inter-faith emphasis is affecting the royal family. If things continue this way it will produce a crisis in the relationship between the Church of England and the State.' A reply by the alleged 'guru', Martin Palmer – director of the International Consultancy on Religion, Education and Culture at Manchester, and an Anglican lay reader – pointing out that he was simply 'an adviser on religion and ecology to the World Wide Fund for Nature' and not in any sense a 'guru' was printed a week later. But this measured and mild reply was buried in the letter columns; the limelight was reserved for the dramatic claims by Mr Higton.

In this instance fundamentalist hostility centred on the issue of co-operation with non-Christian faiths, but there is also a general distaste for environmental concerns. This is based on a fear that they will lead to a concentration upon creation rather than the Creator, and upon the perception that the ecological movement is not restricted to the members of any one faith. The use by Greenpeace of American Indian sayings to emphasize their goals is anathema to fundamentalists. For them, 'the truth is to be found in God's word and not in the fables of American Indians.' (*More Understanding the New Age*, p.7.)

Imputations of pantheism are also utilized to attack 'the explosion in ecology groups and Green Parties' and to link 'New Agers' in general with the atrocities of the Animal Liberation Front, which 'sees no great difficulty in maiming humans to free animals.' (K. Logan, *Paganism and the Occult*, p.102.) Nor is the opposition confined to admitted fundamentalists. In a paper for the Institute for European Defence and Strategic Studies, Andrew McHallam refers to the Green movement's 'hidden dark side, with tendencies towards massive coercion of society, irrationality and paganism.'

He attacks the wide dissemination and acceptance of 'green' views in schools and among the scientific community, and argues that 'the core of deep ecology . . . is a rejection of Christian values in favour of paganism.' But 'most disturbing of all is the illiberal bias of their assumptions' and the fact that some extremists are ready to use 'eco-terrorism'. (*The New Authoritarians*, quoted in *The Independent*, 25 November 1991.)

The common hostility to ecological concern by fundamentalists and prominent right-wing politicians is further emphasized in such public comments as those of John Gummer, former Minister of Agriculture, and the Conservative MP, Teresa Gorman. Mr Gummer, who is a member of the General Synod of the Church of England, has in the past condemned vegetarianism as 'wholly unnatural' because it lacks scriptural authority. But at a London conference of the Food and Drink Federation, in March 1992, he attacked different targets, specifically the European Community ban on BST, a hormone for boosting cow milk yields, and the campaign against food irradiation.

These, he said, were the result of wholly irrational forces that were leading to the 'great danger of the revival of witchcraft.' Precisely how this would come about was not made clear, but his comments were reported under the alarming headline 'Witchcraft threat to food trade.' (*The Independent*, 7 March 1992.)

Mrs Gorman's attack – in the form of a radio broadcast – did not concern the putative religious implications of the Green movement, but it was equally envenomed and made full use of pejorative terms, referring to 'woolly ideas', and 'half-baked science', and describing supporters of the Green movement as 'eco-terrorists.' (*Speaker's Corner*, BBC Radio 4, 16 December 1991.) For fundamentalists it is yet further ammunition, to be stored up with Kevin Logan's emotive link to ALF terrorism.

There is also another element in attacks on the Green movement. A report, issued by the Royal Agricultural Society in 1991, which described organic farming methods as 'uneconomic, unsustainable and unrealistically "Arcadian"', was attacked both by the Prince of Wales – who was disappointed that neither environmentalists nor consumers were involved in its preparation and drafting – and by Richard Young, the development director of the Soil Association. The chairman of the committee who produced the report, Sir Derek Barber, is also a chairman of a subsidiary of Booker, the agribusiness firm, and Mr Young attacked the report's bias, describing it as 'blatant advertising on behalf of the agro-chemical lobby.' (*The Independent*, 26 November 1991.)

It would be quite wrong, however, to suggest that there is any deliberate collusion between multi-national corporations or any other commercial bodies, and fundamentalist bodies or individuals. But it cannot be denied that the thrust of fundamentalist arguments, playing down the importance of creation for the Christian, is also supportive of those companies and governments who have a vested interest in unrestricted exploitation of the Earth's natural resources.

Fundamentalists also condemn unconventional lifestyles, however unalarming they may seem to the world at large. Again, these are dutifully reported in the press. Thus *The Mail on Sunday*, 16 June 1991, reported that fundamentalist medical practitioners were 'waging war on Satan in the surgery' by providing patients with lists of 'Principal Demonic Entry Points'. These included health food shops and vegetarianism.

Even more dangerous is unconventional medicine. Alternative therapies are regularly assailed by fundamentalists who are professionals in the field of health care. It might be noted that they do not complain about allopathy (orthodox medical treatment using drugs to alleviate the symptoms of disease.)

They are often supported, if for non-theological reasons, by the orthodox medical profession. A recent report (*Allergy – Conventional and Alternative Concepts*) by members of the Royal College of Physicians condemns alternative medicine as 'pseudo-scientific' and an irrational waste of time and money. Specifically it condemns homoeopathy as giving no benefit save by means of a placebo effect, and denies that there is any scientific evidence for the beneficial use of acupuncture (a traditional Chinese therapeutic technique which involves inserting fine needles at particular points on the skin) in allergy treatment.

These findings are disputed by other practitioners involved in alternative (or complementary) medicine – and would not necessarily be echoed by fundamentalists themselves. They oppose alternative therapies but do not dispute that they may be effective, although the beneficial effects are alleged to be due to demonic activity – which may be mediated by medical practitioners who are themselves demonically oppressed. Consequently:

> Patients can no longer afford the luxury of failing to determine the spiritual status of those who treat them. Failure to ascertain that may be more costly than a yearly medical bill. Practices that look entirely innocent . . . can become the means of occult bondage. (J. Weldon and Z. Levitt, *Psychic Healing*, Chicago, 1982, p.7)

In the case of acupuncture, the fundamentalist attack justifies itself in a remarkable way. A.D. Bambridge, in his book *Acupuncture Investigated*, 1989, admits that there is no agreement over the physiological mechanisms involved, and suggests either a placebo effect (although, as with homoeopathy, there is no evidence to support this view) or a form of hypnosis as the basis of its action.

But Mr Bambridge's principal reason for opposing acupuncture is non-rational. His starting point is a 'prophecy', spoken by 'a widely-respected medical doctor and pastor of a Malaysian church, Dr Joy Seevaratnum,' and purporting to come from the Holy Spirit. It states that 'Acupuncture was conceived and nurtured by a people who have never known me. It induces a trance-like state in the individual and renders the people vulnerable to varying degrees of oppression and brings me no glory.' (pp.9–10)

On the basis of this, supported by the conviction of ex-missionaries from Korea and a 'Christian doctor' in New Zealand that acupuncture was ungodly and involved 'forces of spiritual evil', Mr Bambridge concluded 'that the Holy Spirit would not have Christians become involved in acupuncture or any other acupuncture related therapy' (p.70). We shall consider the danger of relying on supposed guidance from the Holy Spirit elsewhere. What is most disturbing about this book is that it is one of a popular series designed specifically to attack alternative therapies and 'to keep people who are genuinely seeking truth from error, and to point them to the One who

said, "I am the way, the truth and the life".' It thus arrogates
to itself the imprimatur of Christ in unwarrantably rejecting
a broad sweep of safe and effective methods of healing.

That they *are* safe is not, of course, accepted by all. Although
journalists are occasionally sympathetic to alternative therapies (for example, Charles Oulton, who gave a positive view of
spiritual healing in an article, 'Healing hands reach out to win
credibility', in *The Independent*, 8 February 1992) newspapers
continue to give greater prominence to reports critical of alternative therapies than to those in favour. Duncan Campbell's
attack on the 'Food State' brand of vitamin pills (*The Independent on Sunday*, 28 April 1991), and *The Observer* article, 'Sharp
practice pricks reputation of acupuncture' by Sarah Lonsdale
(15 December 1991), in which the dire consequences described
stemmed from unqualified practitioners rather than from the
practice itself, are typical. The effect on the public is simply
to reinforce the attitudes promoted by Mr Bambridge and his
fellow fundamentalists.

Seeking a malevolent 'spiritual' source of successful therapies,
fundamentalist critics turn most often to practices involving the
mind of the patient. Hypnosis, an artificially induced sleep-like
condition in which the subject is especially responsive to suggestion, is a common target. The mechanisms involved are not fully
understood and this enables fundamentalists to posit a demonic
origin. Thus for Martin and Deidre Bobgan, in *Hypnosis and the
Christian*, Minneapolis, 1984:

> Hypnotism is demonic at its worst and potentially danger-
> ous at its best. At its worst it opens an individual to psychic
> experiences and satanic possession. When mediums go into
> hypnotic trances and contact the 'dead', when clairvoyants
> reveal information which they could not possibly know,
> when fortune-tellers through self-hypnosis reveal the future,
> Satan is at work. (p. 53)

Nor is this all. The use of hypnosis to recall 'past lives' (or to
create them, if one interprets the process as fantasizing from
the subconscious mind) as a means of working out stresses
and anxieties is utterly condemned. The vivid 'memories' of
past lives 'could easily come from demonic spirits influencing
the mind during hypnosis', but it is, in any case, 'obvious

to most Christians that past-lives therapy is demonic.' (pp. 23 and 24.)

So is meditation. All techniques and practices that empty the mind are perceived as dangerous. The state that ensues:

> blinds the mind to the truth of the gospel by displacing reason as a means to truth . . . it opens the mind to false ideas about God and reality . . . opens the personality to demonic incursion. (D. Haddon, 'Meditation and the Mind' in *Spiritual Counterfeits Project, Newsletter*, January 1982, p.2)

And because of its relationship with meditation, Yoga is also condemned. In the pamphlet *What Christians Should Know About Yoga* (Diasozo Trust, n.d.), a conversation is recorded between the author and 'a Christian friend' who says that she 'realized that Yoga was a way for the Devil to gain entry into my life,' and that this could happen 'just through physical involvement.' Because of this the author stresses that:

> The physical exercises cannot be separated from the mental exercises – that is from the meditation; to become involved in either means becoming involved in the forms and ritual of the Hindu religion. The physical exercises in Yoga go far beyond any ordinary exercise course: they are part of a larger whole – Hinduism.

Again there is the implicit link between Hinduism and Satan, with all that implies for inter-racial tolerance.

On a personal level the pamphlet encourages a sense of guilt in the reader, urging him or her to 'confess your sin to the Lord and know his forgiveness,' and to 'renounce all forms of Yoga and turn away from it as a deliberate act of will.' This may seem an absurdity to most readers, but the encouragement to the reader to perceive of Yoga as evil can lead to social disruption, as we shall see (p. 113 below).

But when alternative therapies are designed to bring about changes in an individual's lifestyle that render it more consonant with fundamentalist ideals, they are applauded rather than vilified.

The nuclear family that is the quintessential fundamentalist social unit does not allow room for deviance – especially not for homosexuality – and any sign of tolerance towards sexual behaviour that is tolerated by the law, but that falls outside the 'normal' range, is condemned. Thus the Reverend Tony Higton condemned the *Church Times* as 'a vehicle for homosexual propaganda' (Letter, *Church Times*, 23 February 1990) simply because it advocates tolerance.

There is equally no condemnation for the 'Living Waters Sexual Redemption in Christ' programme, a bizarre system of therapy for homosexuals, whose sexual orientation is seen as due to a psychological blockage. The programme was designed by Andrew Comiskey, a former homosexual, who is pastor of the Vineyard Christian Fellowship in California, and it aims to 'heal' Christian homosexuals so that they become heterosexual.

It is not the first therapy of its kind – several evangelical groups in Britain run 'homosexual healing courses' – but, unlike the others, it has been accepted within the Church of England, and forty-three 'counsellors' are now being trained at the Oak Hill Theological College in London to put the programme into practice with the aid of Mr Comiskey's manual, *Pursuing Sexual Wholeness: How Jesus Heals the Homosexual.* But apart from its potential for a wholly unethical intrusion into private lives, the 'Living Waters' programme can offer far less scientific justification for its practice than can the majority of alternative therapies. It has been described by Dr John Money, an American psychologist who has made a study of such 'healing' courses, as 'a kind of brainwashing. It's similar to a religious cult.' (*The Sunday Times*, 15 September 1991.)

It is also worthy of note that Dr Carey, now the Archbishop of Canterbury, was once a lecturer at the evangelical Oak Hill College. He may be presumed to approve of the programme, for its assumptions and attitudes appear to parallel his own as they have recently been expressed. In March of 1992, Dr Carey was instrumental in preventing the publication by SPCK, the Anglican missionary society and publishing house of which he is the president, of a book of prayers for homosexual Christians. He expressed grave reservations about the contents of the book, *Daring to Speak Love's Name: A Celebration of Friendship*, by Dr Elizabeth Stuart, and warned that he might have to resign as president if SPCK proceeded to publish it. They heeded his warning and the book did not appear.

The tragedy of such actions is that they are interpreted as oppression: the Reverend Richard Kirker, general secretary of the Lesbian and Gay Christian Movement, likened Dr Carey's actions to those of 'an intolerant ayatollah'. They succeed only in further polarizing arguments within the Church about Christian attitudes to homosexuality, and they give comfort to such enemies of tolerance as Mr Higton. His views were reiterated when he argued that Dr Carey should also ensure the censoring of another SPCK publication, *Embracing the Mystery*, which likens the death of homosexual AIDS patients to the Cruxifixion of Christ. 'If the Archbishop is going to be consistent,' said Mr Higton, 'he should ask for the offending section to be removed.' ('Carey in new gay book row', *The Sun*, 16 March 1992.)

Sex is not the only sphere of human activity in which fundamentalists seek to interfere. Every aspect of popular culture is subject to their scrutiny, and much that they see is found wanting. Music, in particular, has proved a fruitful field for fundamentalist hostility.

Not all music, for it has long been recognized as a valuable part of religious services, and during the last twenty years many Christian musicians have promoted what is known as 'Christian Rock' which has the rhythm of rock 'n' roll but with words appropriate to Christian evangelizing. This has been partly in an effort to reach an increasingly alienated youth culture, and partly because they liked popular music – in the manner of the Reverend Rowland Hill who in the early nineteenth century preached a sermon which included the immortal statement, 'The Devil should not have all the best tunes.'

Bob Larson, the American evangelist – and former professional entertainer: 'I wrote it, sang it, and played it' – who is noted for his sermons about the evils of rock music – gave an aesthetic justification for 'Christian' popular music:

'I still like a song with a good rhythm. As a guitar player, Segovia is not the only style I appreciate. But I do draw the line somewhere. When the lyrics explore the obscene and profane, when the entertainers glorify the perverse and forbidden, and when the beat borders on the erotic, that's where I say, 'No!'

He was referring to:

lyrics that present themes of drugs, sex, perversion, and blasphemy, and singers who portray images of sexual licentiousness and drug advocacy. (B. Larson, *Rock*, 1980, p.8)

Larson's argument concerns moral codes, and there are doubtless many of the non-Christian general public who would agree with his strictures. But he also advocates stronger measures against 'secular' rock when it comes within his parameters for rejection. Thus, when one teenager who had listened to a Larson sermon on 'full surrender to Christ' asked for an opinion on his prized six-foot poster of Jimmy Page (of Led Zeppelin), he was told: 'If Christ is really first in your life, tear that poster down today!' After recounting this incident, Larson added: 'If you want God to bless you, get the cursed things [i.e. "unsuitable" records and posters] out of your life!' (*Rock*, p.119). Larson's approach may be more reasoned than the hysterical preachers who urged public burnings and 'trashings' of Beatles records in 1966 (*see* p.100 below) but it is still flawed by attempting to impose a discipline from outside in what must ultimately be a matter of personal choice.

In general terms rock music epitomizes for the fundamentalist all that is undesirable: it emphasizes sexuality, it is brash, noisy and redolent of disrespect for parents and authority of any kind. And while it was born in the American deep South, it is the very antithesis of the more staid hymn-singing of the white evangelicals who epitomize fundamentalism.

But it contained no 'occult' or allegedly anti-Christian elements until the era of the Beatles, whose espousal of Transcendental Meditation and the doctrines of the Maharishi Mahesh Yogi encouraged countless others to follow in their footsteps. All this alarmed and enraged fundamentalists, who saw this path to the East as a certain road to Hell. Not that they anticipated any alternative for the Beatles, for the group had already put themselves beyond the moral pale by their blasphemy in 1966 when John Lennon announced: 'We're more popular than Jesus now.'

Other occult preoccupations of the Beatles were allegedly more dangerous. In 1984 Jacob Aranza published the book *Backward Masking Unmasked*, in which he argued that many recordings of rock music lyrics contained subliminal messages of an offensive, anti-Christian and satanic nature. These messages, he claimed, could be recovered by playing the record backwards; but since it is clearly impossible to play a disc backwards he presumably meant that if it is recorded on tape and then played in reverse, the message will become clear. However one views it, this is a curiously convoluted way of putting across any message deemed to be significant by the singer.

In the case of the Beatles, the subliminal messages began with the song 'Revolution Number Nine' on their *White Album*. Of this Aranza says, 'Played backwards it became "Turn me on dead man, turn me on, dead man . . ." Why? At this time the Beatles were trying to make the public believe that Paul McCartney was dead, merely as a publicity stunt' (p.6). If backward masking *is* possible, other lyrics may be more overtly evil when played in reverse, and their motives may be less self-centred than a simple desire for publicity.

Not that all of them need to be played in reverse. The aim of many rock bands is that their music and lyrics shall shock the public, and to this end it has not been uncommon for them to utilize occult imagery, some of it extremely unpleasant. Thus Led Zeppelin's *Stairway to Heaven* includes the lines 'there are two ways to go, two stairways to face, one to heaven and the other to hell. Me . . . I'll take the second.' To the fundamentalist, choosing Hell may not seem surprising for a group whose lead guitarist Jimmy Page is well known for his enthusiasm for the magician Aleister Crowley, but there is worse . . .

According to the Reverend James J. LeBar, 'Stairway to Heaven' 'has some of the most obvious backward masking, stating quite plainly, that "there's no escaping it. It's my sweet Satan. The one will be the path who makes me sad;

whose power is satan."' (*Cults, Sects and the New Age*, 1989, p.148.) Even if such a subliminal message *is* present, it does not follow that this or any other rock group is advocating devil-worship or is involved in organized Satanism: one must always remember that rock musicians set out to appeal to rebellious youth, and the language (but not necessarily, or even at all, the substance) of Black Magic is an ideal medium for such rebellion.

Fundamentalists, however, make no excuses for the lyrics of rock music. For Peter Anderson, an English evangelist with the Christian Ministries organization: 'Rock music does have very many open and blatant connections with occultism. But there are also the much more sinister dangers associated with what is called "backward masking" on some rock records. (*Satan's Snare*, 1988, p. 63.) He quotes the Led Zeppelin song 'Stairway to Heaven' and refers also to the song 'A child is coming' on the Jefferson Starship album, *Blows Against the Empire*: 'When the tune is played in reverse,' says Anderson, 'the message is quite clear: it says that the "child is a son of Satan".' These and other examples lead him to conclude that, 'Rock music has so many occult overtones that we should avoid it like the plague if we do not want our enemy the devil to get an advantage over us. We certainly should not try to sanitize and harness this musical format as a vehicle for Christian communication' (p.64).

Other fundamentalists are more irrationally strident in their condemnations. Dr Rebecca Brown, in the course of her anti-Catholic book *Prepare for War* (1987), states flatly that rock music 'was a carefully masterminded plan by none other than Satan himself.' Lowell Hart, in *Satan's Music Exposed* (1980), argued that 'rock music is a pollutant every bit as deadly as pornography,' while in England Dianne Core – harking back to hidden messages – claimed that 'the rock groups work subliminally. Heavy rock groups are based on Satanic beliefs. If you play the records backwards, there are Satanic messages.' (*The New Federalist*, 15 November 1988.)

There is also condemnation of 'Christian Rock'. In 1980, Salem Kirban, writing in Lowell Hart's book, *Satan's Music Exposed*, said: '"Christian Rock" is essentially spiritual fornication,' (p.45).

Hart himself condemned it utterly: 'No matter how doctrinally sound the words are, rock, by its nature, can never be used to communicate spiritual truth. Not hard rock, not soft rock. Not any kind of rock. Rock music and godly things just don't go together' (p.107). They were following the lead of an even more intolerant opponent of 'Christian Rock' – the ex-witch, ex-Druid and quondam evangelist, John Todd, who in 1977 declaimed: 'The words may appear to be God's, but the beat belongs to Satan. You tell me, how can they be equally yoked together?'

Throughout the 1970s John Todd (also known as Lance Collins and John Todd Collins) convinced innumerable congregations of American fundamentalists that by his preaching he was exposing a sinister occult plot for world domination (*see* pp.161–2 below). Part of the plot involved rock music. At one of his meetings in 1977 Todd was asked: 'Is rock music an outgrowth of witchcraft?' He replied, 'You can't practise witchcraft without it!' and added apparently convincing personal evidence for his claim: 'Now when I was in there, I was President of the largest booking agency, they have had to change their name since then, because of this publicity I have been giving them, but at the time they were called Zodiac Productions. I knew most of the rock groups in the US. I still do, that is why we live in LA.' Having established his credentials, Todd went on: 'Most of the rock groups are members of a Witchcraft Church! That does not mean they have been initiated, that means that it is their religion. When they write a song, they will ask the witch covens or the Temple to cast a spell over that song so that it will become a hit and sell!' (Transcript of John Todd's Testimony tape, printed in ORCRO 6, pp. 20 and 40–60.) And now comes Satan:

'Now what takes place when a witch casts a spell is they order a lot of demons to do things. They don't know that is what they do, but that is just what happens. Now that means when you go buy an album and you take it home with you, it is like buying a box of crackerjacks. You get a free surprise: it is called a *demon*. It goes along with the record. OK?' He goes on to emphasize that 'it is not the words in the song, it is the music! – witches know this and they hit certain chords on purpose.' And what should be done about rock music? 'When witches get saved, nobody has to tell them to get out of rock music. When they hand their witchcraft items over to be *burnt*, notice I said *burnt*, not thrown into the trash can, it is scriptural, they hand their records over too! because they have lived in a world of the supernatural and they know the supernatural ties in with music' (pp.56–57). Thus the moralizers who gleefully smashed and burned their (or more strictly, other people's) Beatles records in the 1960s found a specious theology, and personal testimony, the more fully to justify themselves. This type of nonsense when given out to individual congregations did not, of course, affect the mainstream of Christian America – and still less Britain; but Todd was taken up and promoted heavily by Jack Chick, and featured in various Chick 'Christian' comics, whose wide distribution has already been noted. The most notorious of these – and one still distributed, even twelve years after Todd's story was shown to be mere fantasy – is entitled *Spellbound*.

The storyline concerns the failed mission of two evangelists who attempt the conversion of a rock star from witchcraft. They learn of the evils of rock music from John Todd (who features in the comic) and they are told in detail how spells are ritually cast upon the mastertracks of records, in order, for example, 'to increase the listeners' belief in reincarnation.' The evil of rock music is centred in the 'spellbinding beat of the druid music' because while 'the words to every song or melody were for casting spells, the drum beat was the key to addict the listener . . . a form of hypnotism. The same beat the druids used is in the rock music of today . . . both hard and soft rock. The beat is *still* there' (p.16).

Blame for the current outbreak of rock was placed, of course, squarely on the Beatles' shoulders: 'The Beatles opened up a Pandora's box when they hit the United States with their druid/rock beat in the 1960s. Then they became so popular that they were able to turn our young people on to the Eastern religions. The flood gates to witchcraft were opened.' The story then leads to a crescendo in which rock music records are burned: 'The most powerful spells hitting Christian homes come through rock music . . . That's why we must burn those records *tonight*' (p.19).

The urge towards destruction is a common and disturbing feature of fundamentalist diatribes against rock music. While it may initially cause no more harm than material loss to the individual who is led to destroy his records, there can be other highly damaging consequences, as we shall see.

Besides rock music, other forms of popular entertainment are also attacked. Some of them are included in a list of indicators of possible occult or satanic activity that was prepared by Sandi Gallant of the San Francisco Police Department. In addition to punk rock music; heavy metal music; . . . posters of heavy metal or punk rock stars', she lists 'graph paper for fantasy games; dice; metal figurines of a mythological nature; posters of mythological beings.' All of these are used in fantasy role playing games, popularly known by the name of the most popular game, 'Dungeons and Dragons', and especially damned by fundamentalists.

In order to play 'Dungeons and Dragons', each player (called an 'adventurer') takes on the persona of a character in the game – warrior, wizard, dwarf, elf, barbarian or supernatural creature, for example – and acts out a fantasy life of swashbuckling adventure, its course determined by the throw of dice and the increasingly complex interaction with other players. It has no board and in order to be satisfactory requires a certain skill at visualization, although small model figures are available that illustrate the various characters. As with any game a certain degree of self-control is also required if it is not to occupy too much of the player's time: adolescents, who are the most frequent players, are not, of course, noted for a desire to avoid spending too much time playing games. Whether such play causes school or other work to suffer depends to a large extent on parental control and responsibility – which are also determining factors in the degree to which children may possibly become obsessed or psychologically disturbed by such games.

But for the fundamentalist it is not a question of 'if' children become obsessed, but 'when', for in their eyes all fantasy role-playing games (but especially 'Dungeons and Dragons') are satanic. In some instances their concern is understandable: Pat Pulling, of Montpelier, Virginia, became an activist campaigning to have 'Dungeons and Dragons' taken off the market after her son Bink committed suicide in 1982 following his obsessive involvement with the game (he had been 'cursed' by another player and the curse evidently left the realm of fantasy and became a reality in his troubled mind). Mrs Pulling came to see the game as so dangerous that in 1983 she founded BADD Inc. (Bothered about Dungeons and Dragons and Other Harmful Influences on Children), and began her public campaign to have it banned. Because of the 'occult' content of 'Dungeons and Dragons' (D & D) she began to read books on occultism and came to believe that a baleful, supernatural influence was at work behind the game.

The initial aim of BADD sympathizers was to have the games removed from schools, but as the organization soon began to flourish in fundamentalist circles, newspaper reports of hostility to fantasy role-playing games began to appear. A typical report is from the *Minneapolis Star and Tribune* of 1 June 1984. It described a meeting held in the First Baptist Church in the town of Bemidji, at which some four hundred fundamentalists raged against D & D. One pastor (the Reverend Larry Forberg) claimed that when rule-books for the game 'say that there is no intended likeness to demonic activity, . . . I would have to say that they are lying or ignorant.'

At the same period a Chick Publications newspaper, *Battle Cry*, was claiming that:

> 'Dungeons and Dragons' instead of a game is a teaching on demonology, witchcraft, voodoo, murder, rape, blasphemy, suicide, assassination, insanity, sex perversion, homosexuality, prostitution, Satan worship, gambling, Jungian psychology, barbarism, cannibalism, sadism, desecration, demon-summoning, necromantics, divination and many more teachings, brought to you in living color direct from the pit of hell!

It is a sad reflection on human gullibility that so many fundamentalists believe this outrageous comment to be true.

In 1989 Pat Pulling published her book *The Devil's Web: Who is Stalking your Children for Satan?* It consists primarily of a catalogue of crimes and suicides in which D & D is alleged to have played a part, together with a series of Appendices detailing such curious subjects as 'Forensic Aspects of Ritual Crime'; 'Signs and Symbols of the Occult'; and 'Glossary of Occult Terms' – all of them inaccurate in varying degrees. Some teenage suicides are undoubtedly of children who were involved or even obsessed with the game, but there is nothing to show that such involvement was a cause rather than a symptom of psychological disturbance, and nothing to justify the extreme terms in which the game is denounced.

English critics of 'Dungeons and Dragons' follow the American line. Thus Peter Anderson, in his book *Satan's Snare*, gives a very detailed, if hostile, account of the game; cites Jack Chick's attack upon D & D with apparent approval; and concludes his account by saying: 'Visualization and the use of the creative imagination are part and parcel of a child's life. But when those faculties are applied in the context of such role-playing games as those I have described, then they can and often do introduce the players to a world of demonic spirits' (p.56). This seemingly reasoned warning is more subtle than the diatribes of Maureen Davies (*see* p.66 above), but it has the same effect: a widening circle of fundamentalists is led to believe in the mythical dangers of the game and encouraged to work for its banning. In the process they must necessarily come to believe that suppressing individual freedom of choice can be a desirable end.

The principal medium by which fantasy is presented to the public is, however, that of film and television. This, too, is a field which excites fundamentalist alarm. Of course, the medium itself is not treated as evil by nature and undesirable films are condemned in the course of those that promote the fundamentalist viewpoint.

The general reasons for condemnation are implicit in Caryl Matrisciana's attack on the film *Gandhi*, with an astonishing attack upon Gandhi himself, in her own video-film, *Gods of the New Age*:

The film *Gandhi* was probably the most effective piece of Indian propaganda to invade the West. It was a political advertisement controlled and heavily financed by the Indian government, and promoted by the peace movement. It propagates a false message of Hindu religious tolerance and non-violence. Historical accuracy was disregarded. Gandhi was no different from most gurus today in that he was a sexual pervert, and was certainly not the non-violent, peace-loving man, as demonstrated in his racial killings of blacks in the Kaffir wars in South Africa. The most important message of the film was that Gandhi was one of the first gurus to link Christianity and Hinduism to form one package, a new religion. I consider him to be one of the fathers of the new age movement.

Other films are attacked in the same video by the fundamentalist author Dave Hunt, who says:

So many of the most popular films today like *Close Encounters*, *Poltergeist*, *ET*, *Return of the Jedi*, *Star Wars* are all based upon Hinduism. For example the force has a dark and a light side, that's black and white magic. The doorway into the occult is an altered state of consciousness. This is the way that Obi Wan Kenobi initiates Luke into the force. He has him working a laser sword, and says your problem is you're trying to think. He puts a visor over his face so he can't see, and he says you've got to tune it out, let the force take over. That's an altered state of consciousness . . . And when he cuts off Darth Vader's head, and it rolls to the ground and he opens the visor to see his own head, that's the most powerful representation of Eastern mysticism you could ask for. The Beatles sang it: 'I am you and you are me, and he is she and all is one.'

Once again the link is made between Eastern religion and occultism. It is forged even more strongly by the comments of Johanna Michaelson (also in the video), who says: 'We are raising an entire generation of children under the bombardment of cartoons and television shows, and fantasy role-playing games and movies that are telling them that the occult and Eastern philosophy is a wonderful thing.'

The dangers of this are stressed by the narrator of the video, who returns to the threat of 'Dungeons and Dragons':

> The minds of children are being trained in the use of the supernatural, and taught the principle of creating what seems like reality through Hindu psycho-spiritual techniques of mind power. 'Dungeons and Dragons', for example, requires participants to mentally murder, rape, torture and otherwise commit mayhem with the aid of occultic powers.'

That the minds of the viewers of this video are equally being affected by a continuous stream of fantastic fictions is not pointed out. Such audio-visual aids are an extremely effective tool for spreading fundamentalist propaganda. But the methods of attacking non-Christian and 'alternative' beliefs and practices are many and varied – and they are often far from pleasant.

SIX

Strategy and Tactics (1)

For fundamentalists to gain popular support for their crusades against alternative medicine, the New Age in general, New Religious Movements, and every other manifestation of what they perceive as demonic intrusions into the world, they must offer some form of proof that such things *are* evil. It is not enough to offer merely their beliefs and opinions as evidence: 'facts' must be produced that are sufficiently convincing, and suitably alarming, to encourage those who do not share the fundamentalist world-view to join with them in promoting persecution and repression.

Of course, they would prefer to vanquish the devil by successful evangelism and the conversion to fundamentalist Christianity of all those who are furthering his work. But this aim will not be achieved by means of what is written on these topics by fundamentalist 'experts'. Much of that is designed for internal consumption only, based on the assumption that the readership is composed of biblical literalists for whom scriptural texts provide adequate warrant for the author's arguments – which will not be the case with those whom they are seeking to convert.

These 'experts' also seek to provide their readers with objective descriptions of the beliefs and practices concerned and with accurate historical and biographical data, in order to equip them for the task of evangelism. But as they contemplate their continuing failure to obtain conversions from among hardened 'cultists', 'New Agers' and other pagans and apostates, so they become more determined that such people and their ways of life shall not be tolerated; what might be described as an 'if-they-won't-join-us-then-beat-them' campaign.

Towards this end propagandist books for the general public are now also being produced. They are no less hostile in tone, but arguments based on biblical authority are less prominent, although by no means absent. An increasing emphasis is placed on carefully selected pejorative reports and comments, in which the common features of 'scare tactic' reporting – innuendo, smear and the specious linking of unrelated events – are all too evident.[1] Whatever their protestations to the contrary, most if not all, of the authors concerned have conducted no original research into the subjects in question and have depended heavily on unreliable secondary sources. As a consequence they remain unaware that many of their 'facts' are fictions, and they continue to make use of them because of their urgent desire to warn the world of its danger and to ensure that the warning is heeded.

But the written word is still primarily for consumption within the fundamentalist community itself: informing, educating, and – especially – helping to mould the attitudes and viewpoint of future leaders of that community. Most fundamentalists are aware that there can be no significant intrusion of their attitudes into the world at large until there is a solid base of convinced and committed church elders, pastors and ministers to whom lay people can turn for information and advice, and who can lead the assault upon the enemy.

There are indications that this foundation has been surely laid. Negative attitudes, founded on errors of fact and false perceptions, have been successfully propagated in both Britain and America. The attitude towards Freemasonry expressed by theological students at Chichester (*see* p. 49 above) is clear evidence of this, as is the absurd public comment about Satanism made by the Bishop of Oxford, the Right Reverend Richard Harries. In the course of a radio broadcast, Dr Harries stated that his own scepticism regarding Satanism had been at least partially overcome because a 'reliable friend' was the source of a claim that 'By the year 2000 Satanists will be sacrificing [around the world] one baby per minute.' (*Ten to*

Eight, BBC. Radio 4, 12 October 1990.) That such a cultured and balanced man can countenance such an idiotic and base-less claim demonstrates the extent to which fundamentalist myths have penetrated the academic world, and it offers little encouragement for those who seek to ensure that reason and truth will ultimately prevail in this field.

The whole question of alleged 'Satanism' is dealt with in Chapter 8, but it should be noted that this example – which is not atypical – focuses on the highly emotive issue of child suffering. It presents a horrifying scenario of a continuing massacre of babies in order to promote spiritual evil. It is also axiomatic with fundamentalists that all the beliefs and prac-tices they condemn are orchestrated by the devil; ergo, all those who are involved in them are thus linked with child sacrifice.

Such horrifying stories are, as we shall see, the stock-in-trade of the peddlers of the myth of Satanism, but they are put to effective use by almost all fundamentalist authors in this field. And it is through raising a clamour about these stories that significant media attention is gained for issues on the fundamentalist agenda. Nor is that attention confined to the written word, although that alone can be effective enough, in mass circulation newspapers and journals, in arousing 'shock-horror' reactions, establishing long-term fear and anxiety, and promoting public hostility. It is just such a cycle that led to the bombing of 'Bridge of Dreams' at Lincoln.

For all evangelical Christians, who place great stress on the importance of preaching, the spoken word is a familiar medium for reinforcing their faith and informing their opin-ions. As a consequence it is utilized extensively in campaigning against the things of the devil, and lectures on such themes – which have a far greater impact and immediacy than does the printed word – are distributed widely. But they are broadcast principally on religious radio channels, which are plentiful enough in America but rare in Britain. Thus sensational claims by John Todd that 'every Bible-believing pastor is on a death list by Satan's crowd'; and by Maureen Davies that 'the Satanists are becoming very violent. In America some of the backslidden Christians are the most prized sacrifices'; and that, 'teenagers are prepared to be murdered and to commit suicide for their belief system in reincarnation,' (Reachout

Trust audio tape on Mrs Davies's American Trip, transcript in *ORCRO 5*, p.36) are less widely circulated here than in the United States of America.

But they are believed, and when those who accept the truth of such claims subsequently present them to the public, with the added impact of visual aids, they appear even more convincing. They can also then be taken up and used by the secular media – in television films of their own devising that build on fundamentalist fantasies and translate them into the folklore of popular culture.[2]

All of which helps to convince the public not only that evil is abroad, but also that the most innocuous of 'occult' pursuits can be the thin end of a demonic wedge. That evidence to this effect is either non-existent or pitifully thin, is explained away by seemingly reasonable arguments – such as that of Maureen Davies who stated, in the course of explaining her attitude to the press:

> You don't hear about these things because this is the type of work we have to do quietly. We don't want the press getting in on to these things because we don't want the situations to be taken out of context, or over dramatized. The things are so bizarre and dramatic enough as it is without having to embroider it up. Yet we need the media to expose it as well, so we need a balance. (American Trip tape transcript, *ORCRO 5*, p.37)

No evidence at all is offered to prove that the alleged threat of human sacrifice (about which she was speaking) has any basis in reality.

And what happens when these things *are* exposed by the media? First, the myths and fantasies are believed; then comments are made opposing tolerance towards unorthodox belief systems – for instance, Russ Parker's complaint against the National Council for Civil Liberties for maintaining that 'witches should have the same rights to practise their religion as adherents of any other system of belief.' 'Since witchcraft is anti-Christian,' he argues, 'it is worrying that such a national society should support it'. (*The Occult – Deliverance from Evil*, 1989, p.11.)

After this the deluge. The implied link between tolerance

and evil provides fundamentalists (and others) with a justification for direct action. It may be subtle and may involve
other motives also, as in the BBC's sudden and costly axing
in March 1992 of the television 'occult thriller', *Moon and Son*,
which featured a professional clairvoyant and her astrologer
son. The ostensible reason was that it had too few viewers
(only 7.8 million), but other low rating series have been
allowed to continue. To outside observers 'it seems strange
that the BBC can afford to lose £750,000 when it is supposed
to be struggling for money.' (*Daily Mail*, 27 February 1992.)
The suspicion remains that undeclared pressure was brought
to bear upon the BBC because of the series' occult content.

Less subtle was the suggestion by Maureen Davies as to how
concerned fundamentalists can protest about television programmes 'of an occult nature'. She suggests that 'Christians',

> . . . ring up and complain. That represents 50,000 viewers.
> We say that if there is three shifts in the complaints depart-
> ment and you rang three times that would be 150,000
> viewers. And if you got two other people to ring and
> complain, and those two got another two, it would have an
> impact. Because these people are only putting programmes
> on which the public are wanting. If the complaints out-
> weighed those that wanted it then they would change the
> programme. It is public demand that puts the programmes
> on the television and we can't afford to be the silent majority
> any more. We have got to start taking action. ('How to
> Deal with the Occult in Your Area', transcript of lecture
> in *ORCRO 7*, p.20)

She also recommends that 'Christians' protest to the managers
of branches of Messrs W.H. Smith in order to stop the sale
of the magazine *Prediction*, which she describes as 'one of the
most dangerous magazines in this country, because it opens
the door for a teenager who doesn't know any knowledge,
about how to able to contact any type of occult activity and
eventually to be able to get into perverted Satanism' (p.20).
There is nothing whatever in *Prediction* – a long-established,
popular monthly concerned largely with astrology and related
subjects – to justify Mrs Davies's description of it, while her

claim that W.H. Smith's had issued a 'national directive' to place *Prediction* with pornographic magazines, and thus out of reach of children, is simply untrue.

But in all of her actions, and in those of her fellow activists, one can discern an underlying strategy. At present it is relatively unorganized, but as cohesive structures (such as BADD and the Reachout Trust) are founded to draw together all those concerned about specific topics, and as individual lectures and hastily arranged protest meetings give way to disciplined conferences organized by those bodies, that strategy begins to take on concrete form.

It is a strategy aimed at bringing about a rejection of all alternative beliefs and practices by the general public. To achieve this goal it is necessary to prevent all positive images of such beliefs and practices from being presented to that public, who might otherwise come to tolerate or even to accept them. This in turn requires that the public be denied easy access to all sources of accurate and objective information that might lead them to such a tolerant view-point. And in bringing this about, the fundamentalist makes full use of the very freedom of expression that he seeks to deny to others.

The basic tactic of fundamentalist activists is that of protest and picket. Notice is served of their opposition to the holding of a specific event, or to the use of specific premises for purposes of which they disapprove, and their opposition is often reported in sensational terms, and with evident relish, by the press. Then demonstrations are held or pickets are mounted – all of which is within the law even though lies and distortions may be paraded before the public.

The protests come even when they are founded on nothing more than rumour, for they still serve the purpose of project-ing negative images. Thus when it was announced in a local newspaper that 'occultists plan to open a shop in Bath' and that the supposed shop 'would sell items used by people who practise the occult, which has long been associated by many with black magic and devil worship. Tarot cards, crystal balls, ouija boards and books on topics including alchemy and fortune-telling would be readily available' (*Keynsham and District Advertiser*, 31 March 1989), reaction was swift. The

Reverend John Raynes denounced the shop in hysterical terms: 'It's dreadful. I liken the occult coming to Bath to giving my son a bottle of Parazone to drink. It's poisonous.' That no such shop was even planned by the minuscule Occult Society (to whom it was attributed) did not affect the gratuitous linking of *all* occult practices with 'black magic and devil worship'. The cause had been served.

Shops specializing in New Age and 'occult' materials are reserved for especial condemnation, but even a hint of unorthodoxy brings hostility. Alan Hooker, the owner of a bookshop at Groombridge in Kent, complained to the press that he had received 'a deputation advising me that it had been reported to them that books on display were "objectionable". No specific cases could be quoted but it seemed that one of the books to which exception had been taken was *Magick* by Aleister Crowley. Although neither of my visitors seemed to have heard of Crowley they felt that being 'occult' it was likely to deprave the local youth.' (*Kent and Sussex Courier*, 11 May 1990.) Subsequent pressure resulted in Mr Hooker removing the book from display. What is perhaps more dismaying is that these self-appointed guardians of public morality had come from Burrswood, a well-known local Christian Healing Centre at one time noted for its tolerance of alternative medicine.

Picketing of Psychic Fairs is also routine – it could be observed at Aberdeen, September 1989, Glastonbury, July 1989, and Bristol, September 1987 – and this, too, is accompanied by alarmist public statements. Visitors to the Psychics and Mystics Fair at Bristol in 1987 were given this warning by Mr G.D. Addison of the evangelical Fellowship of the King group, based in the University:

> I urge anyone who has been to this fair, and feels he or she wants to pursue these things further, to cut all connection with these practices right now. Do not be deceived, and recognize them for what they are: totally evil. The fortune-telling and witchcraft represented at this fair are all highly dangerous and blatantly evil.' (*Bristol Evening Post*, 2 September 1987)

None of these events was prevented from taking place, but

others of a similar nature (in fundamentalist eyes) have been stopped. In Ashburton, Devon, weekly classes in Yoga were banned from the parish church hall because the vicar, the Reverend Peter Gregson, and his parochial church council decided that the activity was 'unchristian' and that 'evil could enter their minds during meditation'. (*The Independent,* 7 December 1991.) This may seem merely petty, but to the twelve women concerned it was both disruptive and hurtful. More unpleasant was the action of the evangelical minister of a Community Church at Beverley in Yorkshire.

In February 1992, John Benyon claimed responsibility for stopping the clinic held by the Association of Healers at a local St John's Ambulance hall. He employed classic techniques. A thirty-strong picket was mounted outside the hall during a spiritualist healing demonstration, and Mr Benyon followed this by telephoning every church minister in Beverley to seek their support for his campaign. 'Catholic, Anglican, Methodist – eleven in all,' he said, 'and all eleven opposed the setting up of a centre for faith healing.' Presumably they agreed with him when he said of the centre: 'Their work is inspired by the devil. They claim to hear voices. I am sure some of these voices are fake, and that those that are not are of the devil.' He used a different argument with the St John's Ambulance Brigade. '[I] explained that if faith healers used the premises it would give medical credibility to something that could only be described as dubious, and in some cases really harmful.' (*Psychic News,* 22 February 1992.) His two-pronged approach was successful and the 'dangerous' healers were duly expelled.

This action, however immoral it might be, was within the law – but on other occasions protest activity has come close to crossing the boundary into illegality. In June 1990 'Christian' protestors at a spiritualist meeting in Liverpool tried to prevent speakers and audience alike from entering the hall where it was held. The medium Albert Best 'went outside to see what was happening. When the Christians saw him they told him what we were doing was not of God but of the devil, and that we were insulting Jesus . . . He was then told he would die within twenty-four hours.' (*Psychic News,* 9 June 1990.) And told it with relish.

Elsewhere, fundamentalists' protest campaigns have inspired

more than verbal venom. In at least two cases they have resulted in arson attacks. The first of these was upon 'The Sorcerer's Apprentice', an 'occult' bookshop in Leeds that also supplies materials ranging from incense to regalia.

This shop was featured in a television programme (*The Cook Report: The Devil's Work*, CTV, 17 July 1989) in which it was presented in a decidedly negative light. Subsequently, on 13 August 1989, the shop was broken into, books on witchcraft and magic were set on fire and the shop was badly damaged. The owner, Christopher Bray, had previously been subjected to newspaper attacks over a period of some eighteen months (commencing with *The Sunday Sport*, 3 January 1988, headed 'Evil – Satanic Guides are Sold to Kids') and condemnation in a speech by Geoffrey Dickens, MP, in the House of Commons. As a consequence, Mr Bray has laid the blame for the attack upon fundamentalists.

It must be said that there is no concrete proof of this, but whoever the perpetrators were, they were undoubtedly inspired by the negative publicity that the shop – a wholly law-abiding business, albeit avowedly 'pagan' in tone – had received during the previous two years. In the other case the campaign of persecution had continued for only one year before it ended in fire-bombing.

The progress of the campaign against the 'occult' shop, 'Bridge of Dreams' at Lincoln, has already been given in outline (*see* pp. 1 and 4–5) but it is worth examining in more detail. Immediately the shop was opened, in December 1990, it was denounced by members of many Christian denominations, and was variously described as 'harmful', 'evil', and 'an ongoing threat'. One protestor stated that 'we do not want this evil in our city', while another 'concerned' individual suggested: 'Let's all make our feelings known and stop this evil shop.' By May the proprietors, Chris and Sarah Townsend, had been driven to close the shop because of 'a hate campaign including death and arson threats, and personal abuse.' (*Lincoln Adscene*, 6 December 1990, 10 January 1991, and 30 May 1991.) When they set up a market stall at Corby they faced a protest campaign by local churchmen, orchestrated by John Celia of the self-styled 'Christian Rescue Service', and returned to Lincoln. Mrs Townsend's new shop was opened in December

1991; on 28 January 1992 it was badly damaged in a fire-bomb attack.

As with the attack on Mr Bray's shop, there is no proof that fundamentalists were responsible for the attack, but demands to 'stop this evil shop' are all too easily taken to heart by disturbed and fanatic individuals. And they could seek justification for their actions in divine hostility to all things occult; a hostility clearly expressed in an earlier letter about the shop from John Shipton and Graham Dealtry, the Area Directors of the Reachout Trust. The letter states:

> . . . it was God who called us, saved us, gave us authority in his name to go and make disciples of people, to help people who ask for help who have been caught up in the many false cults and occult. . . . it is what God says and not what we say or think that matters and God says we should not turn to mediums or wizards, do not seek them out to be defiled by them. (*Lincolnshire Echo* 9 January 1992.)

That Jesus said 'Love your enemies' (Matthew 5:44) they choose to forget.

Elsewhere fundamentalists have attempted to use the law itself to further their own ends. In a very minor way this affected me personally when I spoke at Salem State College, Massachusetts, in May 1990. My lecture was interrupted by the College Police who had been asked by local 'evangelical Christians' to stop my lecture because it was 'satanic'. However, the two troopers who arrived saw no cause for taking any action against an academic lecture on 'The Hermetic Order of the Golden Dawn and the origins of the "alternative" society.' But they did not stay to listen, and they admitted that their view of 'occult' matters was largely derived from the *File 18 Newsletters* (*see* p.167 below and Appendix 4).

More alarmingly, legal prosecutions have been brought against rock musicians, especially those of the 'Heavy Metal' brand – whom fundamentalists consider to be far more danger-ous than either shopkeepers or academics. Thus Pat Pulling of BADD fame believes that the rock star Ozzy Osbourne set out with deliberate, satanic intent to lead impressionable listeners to kill themselves, with his song 'Suicide Solution'.

Osbourne was accused by the parents of nineteen-year-old

John McCollum of being responsible for the boy's suicide by virtue of the lyrics of the song, which, they said, contained subliminal messages not present in the printed copyright version of the song. When Osbourne responded by saying: 'It's absolutely ridiculous to suggest that I'm responsible for their son's death, he was obviously deranged', Mrs Pulling found this to be further evidence of guilt. 'There is a presumption', she says, 'that a victim or perpetrator of a suicide or homicide already was predisposed to violent acts and the music with which he entertained himself was incidental.' The implication being that the opposite is in fact the case.

Mrs Pulling was, nonetheless, obliged to admit (while disapproving of the verdict) that the case against Ozzy Osbourne 'was thrown out of court by Superior Court Judge John Cole who said that holding the musician and his associates responsible for John McCollum's death would inhibit the First Amendment right of free speech.' (*The Devil's Web*, pp. 106 and 108.) In referring to this case, Carl Raschke (*Painted Black*, p.161) notes that McCollum's father sued Osbourne, but he carefully omits to mention that the suit was thrown out, as this would weaken his own case against all that he terms 'Satanism'.

Another case concerned the British band, Judas Priest. In 1985 two youths, Raymond Belknap, twenty, and James Vance, eighteen, shot themselves in a church playground at Sparks, Nevada, after a session of listening to heavy metal music, in particular the Judas Priest album *Stained Class*. Belknap died instantly but Vance survived although he eventually died in 1988 as a result of his wounds. Before his death Vance claimed that he and Belknap had made a suicide pact after listening to *Stained Class*, especially the song 'Beyond the Realms of Death'. Later, a sound engineer, William Nickloff, analysed the album and claimed to find both subliminal messages and backward masking, with such hidden messages as 'Sing my evil spirit' and 'F—— the lord and f—— all of you.' (*The Devil's Web*, p.111.)

Belknap's mother brought a suit against Judas Priest claiming damages of $500,000, and when this came to a hearing at Reno, Nevada, in July 1990, Nickloff's evidence was given in great detail. He was challenged, however, by Timothy Moore, an associate professor of psychology from York University, Toronto who rejected the notion of backward masking.

'The claims simply cannot be substantiated on scientific grounds. It is sheer science fiction,' said Professor Moore, 'I am surprised that these claims have got as far as court. It is absolutely ludicrous to claim that a signal so impoverished as the one in the Judas Priest record can influence a person's actions, let alone when it is hidden amongst all the distractions of the song.' (*The Observer*, 22 July 1990)

The judge agreed with Professor Moore and found for the defendants, taking the view that the two youths – who were both high on drugs and who both had histories of violence and psychological disturbance – were not driven to suicide by the song. What the case did illustrate, however, was that 'rich, well-funded intolerance' could use its muscle 'to destroy anything it considers deviant and unsuitable.' (*The Independent*, 23 July 1990.)

Fundamentalist intolerance can also attempt to destroy character, as with the ridiculous charges brought against prominent evangelical leaders by John Todd. He alleged that Demos Shakarian, founder of the Full Gospel Businessmen's Fellowship, is a leading member of the mythical sect of the Illuminati, and had received $35,000,000 from them; that the witches helped to build Ralph Wilkerson's Melodyland Christian Centre in Anaheim; and that Jerry Falwell (of Moral Majority fame) was 'bought off' with a $50,000,000 cheque. All these men, all leading fundamentalists themselves, denied Todd's claims and were subsequently instrumental in bringing about his exposure.

Todd also attacked 'Christian' rock. Not only is this corrupt, he said, but Pastor Chuck Smith of Calvary Chapel in Costa Mesa, California, set up his Maranatha music company in 1971 and launched 'Jesus rock' music only with the aid of $8,000,000 received covertly from the Illuminati. Smith denied this vehemently and Todd was ultimately discredited. What should be noted, however, is that similar claims against prominent public figures who are *not* fundamentalists, are still believed. When thrown at unbelievers, fundamentalist mud sticks.

But worse than this is the effect of fundamentalist propaganda on pathologically disturbed minds. At its worst it can lead to murder, as in the case of Mark Chapman, who killed the ex-Beatle, John Lennon in December 1980. Some investigators have claimed that Chapman was in some way directed or controlled by the CIA or FBI, but there seems to be little substance to the claim. What is certain, however, is that Chapman was a 'born again' Christian and he is known to have both abhorred rock music and to have been incensed by Lennon's claim that the Beatles were more popular than Jesus. If there had been no sustained campaign of hatred for the Beatles in particular and rock music in general on the part of fundamentalists across America, the seriously disturbed Mark Chapman might not have been driven to commit murder.

As far as is known, none of the wild stories of John Todd ever led any of his avid listeners to kill, although they happily burned records and books. But his stories did fill the minds of his audiences with a disordered jumble of myths and fantasies that have persisted as fact even after Todd's disgrace. But his tales of witches, Druids and the conspiracy of the Illuminati were not his own; they began more than two hundred years ago and were encrusted on even older fantasies about Freemasonry – the most enduring of fundamentalist hate objects.

Appalling though they are to the individuals concerned, the attacks upon small shops and Spiritualist meetings that I have cited have a direct effect upon only a small number of people. To bring home the implications of these attacks for society as a whole it is necessary to become aware of what can happen when suspicion, fear and hatred are directed at larger institutions. In the case of Freemasonry, every one of its members around the world is potentially under threat from the enemies of the freedoms of expression and belief.

There is no evidence to show that current fundamentalist hostility to Freemasonry has led to demonstrations, legal action, kidnapping, fire-bombing or murder, although in the past Freemasons have suffered from the actions of secular authorities who have manipulated fundamentalist myths and fantasies for their own ends. Examining how this came about provides a valuable object lesson in applied intolerance, and illustrates clearly the dangers to society that follow the fusion of factual ignorance and religious bigotry.

Examples of the comments of hostile writers on Freemasonry have already been given, but few of them are as comprehensive in their denunciation as Ankerberg and Weldon, whose study *The Secret Teachings of the Masonic Lodge* (1990) has already become a handbook for fundamentalists. They state that Masonry is a potentially occultic religion and opens the doors to the world of the occult. Masonry encourages the pursuit of the occult in five different ways: (1) Masonry accepts the premise of the New Age and modern parapsychology concerning latent human potential – the development of allegedly 'natural' psychic abilities; (2) Masonry bears a striking similarity to many other occult arts; (3) Masonry encourages the individual Mason to pursue its 'esoteric truths'; (4) Masonry is related to mysticism and may encourage the development of altered states of consciousness; and (5) many Masons are working for what can only be termed 'occult Masonry' (p. 216).

Not one of these statements is true, and not the slightest evidence is offered to support them. But they are believed to be so by fundamentalists who read the book. Elsewhere (pp. 232 and 233) the authors condemn Freemasonry because of its 'cultic characteristics'; 'its ability to intrude into the church'; and because it furthers 'the cause of paganism, mysticism, the psychic, and the occult.' All of which they also condemn.

None of this is new. Soon after modern Freemasonry was institutionalized, in 1717, Pope Clement XII issued the Bull *In Eminenti* (1738) in which, for reasons mirrored by those of Ankerberg and Weldon, he 'condemned and prohibited' the 'depraved and perverted' society of Freemasons. As a consequence of this attack a number of Freemasons were imprisoned and tortured in Italy, Spain and Portugal.

Over the course of the succeeding two centuries it was followed by a long series of further papal condemnations, the most furious and reactionary of which was *Humanum Genus*, issued by Leo XIII in 1884. This denounced Freemasonry – together with such evils as secular education, the separation of Church and State, and the very idea of democracy (all recognizable as evils in the eyes of today's

Protestant fundamentalists also) – as being an active part of the 'kingdom of Satan', bent on violent revolution and the destruction of religion, under the guidance of 'hidden and unknown chiefs.'[3]

The roots of such vehement Catholic opposition lie in ignorance and the consequent fear of the unknown. In the early eighteenth century the Catholic Church was frightened both by the tolerance implicit in the ideas and ideals of the enlightenment, and by the explicit embracing of tolerance by Freemasonry itself. By the end of the century the Church had become further alarmed by the appearance of the Order of the Illuminati – a quasi-masonic Order whose power and influence existed solely in the imagination of its creator, Adam Weishaupt, but which came to be seen as a force behind the French Revolution.

The publication of two popular works claiming to justify the link brought a budding anti-Masonry to the Protestant world also (John Robison, *Proofs of a Conspiracy*, 1798; and Abbé Barruel, *Recollections . . . for a History of Jacobinism*, 1797). And upon this has been built the myth – propagated by Roy Livesey and John Todd among others – of the Illuminati as a Jesuit-dominated, all-powerful, occult group manipulating global finances and politics in order to further the cause of Satan.

Before his lies were exposed, John Todd claimed to have been a member of the ruling 'Council of Thirteen' of the Illu-minati, and stated that among their objects was the murder of prominent Christian ministers, because the Illuminati felt that 'they are better dead than alive, and were willing to spend millions of dollars to make sure that it happens.' He also linked the Order to Freemasonry and roused hostility to such a pitch that US Senator J. Strom Thurmond, a former Governor of South Carolina and a prominent Freemason, was expelled from the board of the fundamentalist Bob Jones University in Texas. (*Christianity Today*, 2 February 1979.)

Roman Catholic hostility was further stirred up in the 1890s by the 'revelations' of 'Leo Taxil' and his collaborator 'Dr Bataille' (pseudonyms of the French journalists, Gabriel Jogand Pages and Charles Hacks). These purported to describe the doings of 'The New and Reformed Palladium', a supposedly vehemently anti-Christian Luciferian

Freemasonry involving blasphemy, sacrilege, human sacrifice and ritualized sex, for which purpose it admitted both men and women. Absurd though the stories were – they included an obliging personal appearance by the devil, in the form of a demon crocodile, to play the piano at a masonic soirée – they were widely believed by the Catholic authorities. Eventually Pages brought his hoax (for such it had been) to an end; he had failed to produce in the flesh his protégée, Diana Vaughan, a supposed satanic convert to Rome, and instead, in April 1897, he announced at a public meeting in Paris that the whole affair had been designed to discomfit the Church.[4]

But the myth of the Palladium survived, largely because anti-Masons wished to believe it, and partly because Taxil based his nonsense on a real masonic body: the Ancient and Accepted Scottish Rite of Freemasonry, based at Charleston in the USA, and at that time presided over by Albert Pike, a former Confederate General and the most influential figure in American Masonry during the nineteenth century. Pike was a prolific author, but apart from his idiosyncratic masonic instructional manual, *Morals and Dogma* (1871), his works are little known and mostly difficult of access. As a consequence, when a fictitious 'Official Notice' by Pike, purporting to be 'Instructions' advocating the worship of Lucifer, was published in 1894, anti-Masons were all too ready to believe that it was true. Even today this fiction is maintained and the link made between Freemasonry and Satanism. Thus, the Reverend Steve Morgan of Merthyr Tydfil can say, 'There is evidence to suggest that in Freemasonry at its highest point, the Great Architect is named as Satan . . . I know two masons who have left their lodge as a result of that knowledge.' (*The Western Mail*, 14 August 1989.) That evidence, which he does not give, can only be the lies about Albert Pike. But relying upon a lie to uphold an article of faith is a dangerous practice, with damaging consequences to that faith, as we shall see in due course. For the present let us carry forward the anti-masonic movement.

After World War One there were many in Britain and America, with fundamentalist Christians prominent among them, who could not accept that the Russian Revolution was the result of social forces. Because it was not only

Communist but also atheist, they saw it as part of a wider Jewish-Masonic plot against Christian civilization, and wrote hysterical denunciations of it.[5] These theories helped to foster the virulent anti-masonry of Nazi Germany that led to the suppression of Freemasonry in occupied Europe and to the deaths in concentration camps of many hundreds of Freemasons. And yet they are still promoted today.

The specifically anti-Jewish element is less evident, but the smear of Satanism remains, spreading from religious anti-masonic literature to the purely secular variety, where financial profit rather than religious fanaticism is the motive. Authors in both camps feed off each other's fantasies. Thus Martin Short, in *Inside the Brotherhood* (1989), quotes the Pike 'Instructions' but states that 'its authenticity is in doubt' while further claiming that 'the quote sounds authentic.' He then suggests that Freemasonry has been subtly influenced by such occult bodies as the Golden Dawn, by Aleister Crowley, whose 'views on the devil', he says, 'were astonishingly similar to those attributed to . . . Albert Pike' (p.136).

Where this nonsense comes from he does not say, but it returns to the fundamentalist fold in Ankerberg and Weldon, and in Ian Gordon's *The Craft and the Cross* (1989). The general public received it via the hostile and one-sided television series based on Mr Short's book. They were not treated to all the tales with which readers were regaled in the book itself – especially not to the book-burning episodes that so epitomize the fear and hatred underlying fundamentalist intolerance.

In one of these, an un-named ex-Mason, a 'leading City of London financier' had felt 'an overpowering presence of evil' during the ceremony in which he was raised as a Master Mason, accompanied by 'a piercing pain in my skull'. These headaches, and other ills, recurred for many years until he followed the advice of a Pentecostalist minister who saw in a supernatural manner that the 'source of the evil' was the man's masonic regalia and ritual books. When these were duly burned he was freed from his suffering. This seems to cast the minister in the role of witch-doctor, and suggests the working of primitive superstition rather than the Christian faith. Similar cases, equally dubious in theological terms, are recounted in David Vaughan's *The Diary of a Freed Mason*, and in John Lawrence's *Freemasonry – a Religion?* (1987). What is most disturbing about them is the relish with which the act of destruction is described and the implicit blasphemy in the specious justification – in one instance it is carried out on the alleged authority of 'the Holy Spirit'.

But while this folly may be shrugged off, far more unpleasant allegations about the nature of Freemasonry have also been made. They are emotionally highly charged and involve, once again, the supposed threat to children. The most pernicious was made by Dianne Core, the founder of Childwatch (an organization dedicated to rescuing children at risk of abuse) In a speech delivered at Rome in 1989, she made a series of monstrous and wholly unsubstantiated accusations linking Freemasonry to child abuse:

> I also accuse the masonic, the Freemasonry groups. These men have sold themselves to the devil! That's why it is so difficult for us to get to the bottom of who abuses these children. If these men are Freemasons they are protected by their very position in society. . . . Freemasons have sold their souls to the devil and many Freemasons are corrupt and protected by the Freemasonry and that's why the workers who try to protect these children, particularly from Satanism and any kind of paedophilia are constantly in danger. (Transcript of speech printed in *ORCRO 4*, p.25)

Out of this nonsense have come solemn media reports that treat the allegations seriously, as in *The Observer* of 16 February 1992: 'Survivors also allege that a masonic-style network of senior doctors and police officers are involved in cults.' Not a direct accusation, but the subtle smear which encourages public antipathy to Freemasonry. The next stage will be a repetition of the old stories of kidnap and murder, which are founded on an historical event.

In 1826 William Morgan, an itinerant bricklayer, living at Batavia in upper New York State, fell out with his fellow Freemasons and announced that he would publish the texts of all the masonic rituals. In a misguided attempt to prevent this, a number of local Masons abducted him, and although Morgan was never seen again no evidence at all has ever been produced to show that he was murdered. His kidnappers admitted the abduction and were duly punished but they all strenuously denied murder, and Morgan seems to have been bribed to leave America (for which there *is* evidence). But innuendo is a powerful weapon of intolerance, and their folly placed it in anti-masonic hands. It has been used ever since to ill-effect – adding the crime of murder to the sin of Satanism in what fundamentalists perceive as the 'cult' of Freemasonry.

They may denounce Freemasonry, but they cannot take legal or social action against it without state support, and that – at present – is improbable in the Western world. But illegal action is another matter, and while it has never been used against Freemasons, kidnapping is a tactic that has been employed in connection with the members of other 'cults'. However, 'abduction' is an ugly word and it is sanitized into 'rescue'. Yet again, the justification is the supposed threat to the young and innocent.

NOTES TO CHAPTER SIX

1. Examples of this type of work are Cole, M. et al, *What is the New Age?* 1990; and Logan, K. *Paganism and the Occult*, 1988. The latter is described on its cover as 'A manifesto for Christian action'.
2. An example is *Devil Worship: the Rise of Satanism*, Jeremiah Films, 1989. The English version of this film, which is introduced by Caryl Matrisciana, contains material utilized in Channel 4 TV documentaries about alleged Satanism.
3. For the texts of the Papal Bulls against Freemasonry see Alec Mellor, *Our Separated Brethren the Freemasons*, 1969.
4. For the Taxil affair *see* Eugene Weber, *Satan Franc-Macon: Le Mystification de Leo Taxil*, Paris, 1964; and H.T.F. Rhodes, *The Satanic Mass*, 1954.
5. Examples are, Nesta Webster, *World Revolution*, 1922, and *Secret Societies and Subversive Movements*, 1924; C.M. Stoddart, *Light-bearers of Darkness*, 1930, and *The Trail of the Serpent*, 1936; Lady Queenborough, *Occult Theocrasy*, 1933. The source of their fantasies was *The Protocols of the Learned Elders of Zion* (English trans. 1922), a wholly fictitious document that set out the stages of the alleged 'Jewish Plot'.

SEVEN

Strategy and Tactics (2)

On 21 May 1984, the following report appeared in the *Western Daily Press* newspaper:

> Bristol's Euro MP Mr Richard Cottrell flies to Strasbourg today to present a report dealing with cults like the Moonies. Mr Cottrell's report – which has taken nearly three years to prepare – is due to go before the vote of 434 Euro MPs after a long debate scheduled to begin this evening. The main proposal is for a voluntary code in which the cults would police themselves. This aims to overcome many of the bitter complaints, including brainwashing, breaking up of families and even criminal activities such as prostitution and child abuse.

The 'bitter complaints' were guaranteed to arouse public alarm, especially those which implied threats to children and to the family. But there was nothing in the press report to indicate anything other than a laudable concern on Mr Cottrell's part for securing the basic right of the individual to freedom from oppression. That the foundations of oppression and persecution from another direction would have been firmly laid had Mr Cottrell's Report and his related parliamentary motions been taken to their logical conclusions was not suggested. It is probable that this did not occur to the newspaper staff. The fundamentalist hand in the whole affair had not been revealed.

Parental alarm over their children's involvement in extremist cults began to grow in the 1970s when 'a major expansion in cult recruitment of middle-class youth began'. (J.C. Ross and M.D. Langone, *Cults: What Parents Should Know*, 1988. p.2.) But definitions of a 'cult' depended largely on who was defining it; for many parents a cult was any organization or group that, in their eyes, was alienating their children from them. This is far too broad a definition, for it could include any well-established religious faith or political creed which parents rejected or disapproved of. It could also include any of the more recently established offshoots of the major religions, or any of the many 'alternative' belief systems. These are generically described as 'New Religious Movements', and although *all* cults of today can be so described, the terms are not interchangeable.

Hostility to cults is more properly directed at those which are destructive or extremist. The identifying features of these have been set out by the Interfaith Coalition of Concern about Cults. They are as follows:

> A destructive cult has a self-appointed messianic leader who focuses followers' veneration upon him or herself, claims divine selection, and exercises autocratic control over members' lives. Deception and misrepresentation are used for purposes of recruitment, retention and fund-raising. Techniques are used that are aimed at controlling individual thought and personal privacy, frequently leading to a coerced reconstitution of personality. (J.J. Lebar, *Cults, Sects and the New Age*, 1989, p.15.)

Few would dispute that membership of such cults would be socially, mentally and spiritually damaging. But the problem constantly arises of determining whether or not any given cult truly fits that pattern. For the fundamentalist, the very existence of the cults is proof of the devil's success; thus, because of the 'influence of the occult spiritual community', 'TM is virtually a household word, particularly in America, and through it, Satan has almost succeeded in establishing a "vision of possibilities" particularly suited to the mainstream cultural predisposition.' (SCP Pamphlet, 'A Preliminary Blueprint for Discernment', quoted in R. Enroth, *Youth, Brainwashing and the Extremist Cults* 1977, p.219). And 'cult' is a pejorative word to be applied to any movement or belief system that is perceived as demonic.

Its use in this way is exemplified by Walter Martin, for whom every part of the New Age movement is a cult, and 'The [New Age] cult is the world of occultic darkness and spiritual danger beyond belief.' (W. Martin, *The New Age Cult*, 1989, p.8.) It is this perception of spiritual danger, as much as the alleged threat to the family, that arouses fundamentalist fear and hostility. But in order to turn public opinion against the cults – *all* cults – the dangers to children and family are especially stressed.

Following the rapid growth of widespread parental concern in the 1970s, organizations were founded to combat the perceived threat from the cults. Among the most prominent is the American Family Foundation (AFF) which was founded in 1979. It is a non-profit research and educational organization that collects, analyses and disseminates information on cults and on 'manipulative techniques of persuasion and control'. The AFF is also non-denominational, as is the Cult Awareness Network (CAN) which was set up in Chicago by the Citizens' Freedom Foundation. CAN is 'dedicated to promoting public awareness of the harmful effects of mind control [but] confines its concerns to unethical or illegal practices and does not judge doctrine or belief.' (J.C. Ross and M.D. Langone, *Cults What Parents should know*, 1988, p.129.)

In England the most significant body is Family Action, Information, and Rescue (FAIR), which was founded in 1975, ostensibly as a parents' organization which provided enquirers with facts about cults and sects. FAIR produced a quarterly newsletter updating the activities of numerous New Religious Movements, and organized annual conferences, with guest speakers who reported on the progress of the anti-cult movements in the US and elsewhere. It also participated in international conferences relating to the problem of cults.

The first of these was held in December 1980 at Paris, where the 'Association pour la Défence de la Famille et de l'Individu' (ADFI) organized a conference attended by some sixty people from fourteen different countries. The purpose of the conference was for participants to discuss 'the proliferation of new multinational organizations commonly called today the "new sects", which are in fact totalitarian ideological and religious organizations.' (*ADFI Communiqué*, January 1981.)

After the conference a 'declaration' was issued, condemning the cults and announcing the formation of an international association, the 'Comité International', which would bring together appropriate associations from Austria, Belgium, Canada, Denmark, England, France, Germany, Greece, Holland, Japan, Scotland, Spain, Switzerland, and the USA. England was represented by FAIR.

The 'declaration' stated that the 'Comité' 'will not be able to promote any particular religious belief.' In practice it did not function quite in this way. The five elected members included Kenneth Frampton, chairman of the evangelical Deo Gloria Trust; Dr Johannes Aagaard; and Pastor F.W. Haack – all of whom were involved in making the film *Gods of the New Age* (*see* p.77 above). FAIR's representative at the conference was Caryl Williams – who was also involved with the Deo Gloria Trust. Given the stance of all those involved, it is almost inconceivable that the Comité could be neutral in matters of faith.

Indeed, the publicity branch of the Deo Gloria Trust, Deo Gloria Outreach, was already actively involved in promoting international co-operation in countering the cults. The issue of *News & Views*, the Deo Gloria newsletter, for March 1980, clearly stated that 'During the last few years one of our purposes has been international co-ordination, linking together and introducing those concerned in various aspects of cult exposure.'

That purpose had found practical expression in May 1977, at a conference entitled *The Challenge of the Cults*, held at the Belgian Bible Institute, at Heverlee in Belgium. Secrecy was a keynote of the conference, and participants were told: 'Your attendance at this conference will constitute an obligation not to disclose its proceedings but to treat them as confidential.' Reports of the various sessions – which included such themes as: The devil's common strategy of deception; Brainwashing techniques; De-programming and the law; The Christian approach to the cults and training required; and Search and rescue – were labelled 'confidential and are NOT for distribution.'

One reason for this was probably the positive view promoted of de-programming (that is reversing the process of 'brainwashing' that cult members allegedly undergo). It was not praised and its faults were pointed out – it has 'nothing to do with evangelism, and nothing to do with salvation', and 'deprogramming involves illegal, unethical and forceful methods. Brutal tactics are rampant' – but what was emphasized was that, 'Deprogramming works, and does break these thought chains.'

A second conference, entitled *The Challenge of the Cults*, was held at Hoddesdon in Hertfordshire, in June 1978. As with the conference in Belgium it was not open to the press or the public. It alarmed Muslims, Hindus and more tolerant Christians, and their fears were articulated by the press. *The Guardian* reported that, 'Organised by the Deo Gloria Trust, in association with the Evangelical Alliance, the conference will debate "means whereby the public may be alerted, the cults exposed, and their victims restored to sanity,"' and noted that 'The themes of the conference sound aggressive, with sections on "Spiritual warfare and victory in Christ" and "Guidelines to distinguish cults from Biblical Christianity".' (M. Walker, 'Churches fear wave of cult witch-hunts' in *The Guardian*, 13 June 1978)

What was being sought at such conferences was academic support for the argument that conversion to cults was linked with some diagnosable form of mental disorder. In 1981 it was obtained. At Bonn, in Germany, another conference, on *The Effects of New Totalitarian Religions and Pseudo-Religious Movements upon Society and Health*, was held under the auspices of the German 'Association of Parents' Organizations'. Among three speakers on the psychiatric problems related to cult membership was Dr John Clark of the Harvard Medical School, who spoke on 'Destructive Cult Conversion'.

Dr Clark's views on diagnosing cult members as mentally ill were not, however, generally accepted by the medical profession. At a meeting held on 16 November 1979, the Complaint Committee of the Board of Registration and Discipline in Medicine, at Boston, Massachusetts, discussed a complaint filed by the Citizens' Commission on Human Rights (a body sponsored by the Church of Scientology, a prime target of anti-cult activists) concerning Dr John G. Clark.

Some three years earlier Clark had, 'diagnosed as mentally

ill' a Hare Krishna devotee, and it was about this diagnosis that the complaint was made. The Committee decided against formal disciplinary action, but stated, in a letter to William P. Homan, Jr., the Citizens' Commission attorney, that:

> ... we do want to draw your attention to two items in the record that are troubling ... we note that there is no recognized diagnostic category of mental illness of 'thought reform and mind control'. Moreover, the basis on which this 'diagnosis' was made seems inadequate, as mere membership in a religious organization can never, standing alone, be a sufficient basis for a diagnosis of mental illness.'

They further noted that: 'It is also improper and unlawful to base a finding of mental illness solely on membership in a religion regardless of one's personal opinion as to the merits of that religion.'

Despite this, Dr Clark was still invited to speak at anti-cult conferences, together with other psychologists and psychiatrists who shared his view. In 1984 he received the Leo J. Ryan award, that is 'presented annually to the person or persons judged most active in focusing public attention on the dangers of destructive cults.' He was described in the *Cult Awareness Network News* for October 1984, as 'an internationally known authority on destructive cults. He has treated hundreds of former cult members and their families. Dr Clark is the Assistant Clinical Professor of Psychiatry at Harvard Medical School and is chairman of the American Family Foundation's Executive Committee.' This says little for the objectivity of the AFF, but the effect of Dr Clark's work has been to gain wide public acceptance for the specious link between mental illness and cult conversion. It would be used widely to justify dramatic and illegal action, but anti-cult activity also entered the political sphere.

Richard Cottrell's attempt to have anti-cult legislation (initally in the form of a 'voluntary code of conduct' for cults and sects) passed by the European Parliament ultimately failed, but while his campaign was active, from 1982 to 1984, it aroused considerable alarm, not only among the cults but also within major Christian denominations and within other faiths. In mid-February 1984, the French Protestant Federation, sent a letter to all MEP's condemning any official interference in religion and asking all MEPs to 'oppose an initiative which could have harmful consequences and which offers no positive solution to the problem in question.' This uneasiness appeared to be justified when Mr Cottrell commented to the Dutch Newspaper *Trouw*, in March 1984, that 'The sects are intolerant and therefore don't have any reason to complain that we are intolerant with them.'

More disturbing was the support that Mr Cottrell obtained from politicians in England. Neil Kinnock, then leader of the Labour Party, was quoted as saying that 'the methods used by the various "destructive cults" reduced followers to automatons and had to be fought in every legitimate way,' while Gerald Kaufman, then Shadow Home Secretary, was reported as stating that 'the next Labour Government would seek stringent use of immigration regulations to deal with representatives of cults who came from abroad in order to safeguard the young.' (*Hull Daily Mail*, 6 April 1984.)

Opposition to the campaign was voiced by the British Council of Churches; the Islamic Council of Europe; the Irish Council for Civil Liberties; and by Sikh, Hindu and Christian bodies within Mr Cottrell's own constituency. Eventually the threat of restrictive legislation was removed, but fundamentalist hostility to the New Religious Movements remains, and the eagerness of politicians to take up illiberal causes for reasons of expediency should not be overlooked.

The constitutional position in Britain and Europe remains that of tolerance to all religious bodies that act within the law. Children are protected under the law and cult recruiting activity must be confined to adults – which in practice it always has been. But those who are utterly opposed to all cults stress the threat to the young; the American Family Foundation handbook, *Cults: What Parents Should Know*, is subtitled *A practical guide to help parents with children in destructive groups* – even though the 'children' are adults.

It should also be noted that there are well-established mechanisms to protect the young and the incompetent, but even these are deemed inadequate by some anti-cult bodies. There were many attempts during the 1970s and 1980s to introduce legislation in a number of American States that would extend such conservatorship and guardianship provisions so that parents could legally restrain their adult children and attempt to break the hold that the cults are alleged to have upon them. (*See* F.K. Flinn, 'Criminalising Conversion' in *Crimes, Values and Religions,* 1985.) So far all such attempts have failed, and parents who remain convinced of the urgent need to extricate their children from whatever cult they may have joined have turned instead to professional deprogrammers.

These are often ex-cult members who have themselves been deprogrammed and who are intimately aware of the beliefs and practices of the cult concerned. This is a decided advantage in their work as it enables them more effectively to arrange the kidnap that inevitably precedes the deprogramming. Almost every stage of the process is illegal and although the unpleasant nature of some extremist cults is such that one feels sympathy with parents driven to extreme measures, the illegality cannot be overlooked.

Most 'cult' members who are subject to kidnap and deprogramming are adults who have freely chosen to enter the cult and have not been forcibly detained within it. Nor, save in rare instances, have they been 'brainwashed' by cultists. They may have been dissatisfied with their previous lives and a desire to escape from loneliness, insecurity and religious doubt may have been factors involved in their conversion to specific cult beliefs. But this does not justify violent 'rescue'. A reasoned response to the problem of cult membership is to attempt a healing of any underlying intra-familial conflicts that may have precipitated conversion, and to use rational argument to combat cult beliefs. But the extremism of fundamentalist attitudes to all cults – condemning them indiscriminately as satanic – has led many parents to feel inadequate to the task.

But deprogramming can be far more damaging to both parents and cult members than simply maintaining the status quo. It is also an extremely expensive process, for deprogrammers charge very high fees, and parents may not realize the level of violence involved. The kidnappers themselves rarely suffer. Thus Martin Faiers and David Gregory, of the deprogramming organization Council for Mind Abuse, 'walked free from a Swiss court – after kidnapping a Hare Krishna disciple at gunpoint . . . The court in Lugano had heard that Passera, twenty-four, had been handcuffed, gagged and forced to stay awake and watch videos after being snatched at gunpoint.' (*Western Daily Press*, 26 November 1990.) One reason for this virtual immunity is the extremely negative attitude to cults maintained by the courts; an attitude engendered by media hostility which stems in turn from the biased view of cults presented by such bodies as the Deo Gloria Trust.

There can, of course, be no defence for the practices of some cults, and it is not my aim to defend any of them. But if freedom of belief and worship are not to be eroded, then all belief systems whose practices fall within the law must be permitted free expression – which includes the right to proselytize. This is not a right that is always recognized, and in some instances it is denied even to major denominations. As in the cases of Debbie Gudgeon and the Reverend Philaret Taylor, both of whom were converts to Catholicism.

At the age of seventeen Philaret Taylor converted to the Old Catholic Church and became a monk, but his parents disapproved of this conversion and in July 1976, when he was twenty-two years of age, the now Reverend Taylor was abducted from the Monastery of the Holy Protection of the Blessed Virgin Mary, in Oklahoma City. In strict terms the abduction was technically legal because the parents had secured a court order allowing Mr Taylor Snr 'temporary guardianship' of his son.

But this had been obtained on very dubious grounds. In an affidavit duly sworn on 12 August 1976, the Reverend Taylor stated that the court proceedings were 'without notice' and that he was not allowed to be represented by the lawyer of his choice on the grounds that he was a member of the same religious order. Further, the psychiatric evidence of a supposed illness that enabled the parents to obtain the temporary guardianship of their son which they sought was seriously flawed. Philaret Taylor stated, in his affidavit, that

'Kevin M. Gilmartin, a clinical psychologist from Tucson, Arizona, submitted a letter offering professional psychological support for the proceedings without ever having seen or examined me.'

Worse was to follow: 'I was threatened with commitment to a mental institution if I did not cooperate and renounce my religion.' Eventually the Reverend Taylor escaped from the captivity of his family and returned to his monastery, while the court order placing him under the temporary guardianship of his father was declared invalid. But not before his deprogrammers had abused him: 'They asked me if I would take off my robe, and I said "no", for a priest never takes off his habit, so they ripped it off, along with the cross I wore'. (Interview in *The National Courier* December 1976.)

Debbie Gudgeon's story was reported in *The Washington Post* of 3 December 1976. She had been taken from a Roman Catholic community in Orangeville, Ontario, by members of her family and taken to the home of a family friend where, she said, a deprogramming team worked on her for fourteen hours. She escaped, however, and returned to Bethany House, her religious community. The abduction was quite illicit – she was twenty-three years of age – but the deprogrammer, Ted Patrick, escaped prosecution because of the unwillingness of his victim to deepen the rift with her family.

Miss Gudgeon became a Roman Catholic when she was at college, and moved into a house with about ten other Catholics to form 'an alternative Christian community'. Her Protestant parents objected and opposed her decision to pursue social work within this community rather than to continue her studies or obtain a job. But their attempt at 'rescue' and deprogramming failed and only further damaged relations with their daughter.

Not all deprogramming is carried out on religious cult members. Susan Wirth was not a member of a religious cult, nor was she a teenager or young adult when, in July 1980, she was forcibly abducted from her home in San Francisco by a group of men acting on behalf of her mother. She was then a thirty-five-year-old college professor with a doctorate. Her crime in her mother's eyes was to belong to 'leftist political groups that are neither violent nor cultist'. (*The Independent*, Long Beach, Ca., 21 July 1980.)

A year before, Susan Wirth had left her teaching job in Pennsylvania, feeling that her parents were 'suffocating' her, and moved to California. There she became involved in various radical – but not extreme – causes, and had friends who seemed 'too liberal' to her mother. Eventually Mrs Wirth became convinced that her daughter had been 'brainwashed', and began to attend monthly meetings of the Personal Freedom Association which met at a local church. This was, 'a small group of about 100 parents whose children have joined religious cults. Members said the group included no deprogrammers, but that it does hire deprogrammers to "rescue" their children.' She then set about arranging for her daughter's beliefs to be changed – at a cost of $10,000 from the family savings.

The attempt failed; there was no healed relationship between mother and daughter, and the only beneficiaries were the deprogrammers, and the unreasoning fundamentalist critics of 'cults' who feel no guilt at the tragedies which they have indirectly caused – tragedies which are not lessened in depth whatever the beliefs of the victim of deprogramming.

The basic immorality and nastiness of the kidnapping and deprogramming of 'cult' members is illustrated by the story of Bernadette Bradfield, a twenty-two-year-old convert to the Hare Krishna movement. In February 1983, Miss Bradfield was 'unlawfully imprisoned at a cottage in North London' and subjected to deprogramming by John Mathewson (an ex-Hare Krishna member) and others, including members of her own family. After four days she was released, and made a long statement about the kidnap (the second she had made; in the first, to the police, she had given a false account in order to protect her mother and other relatives who were involved in the kidnap).

Bernadette Bradfield's statement of 12 February 1983 was given, she said, because, '. . . I felt impelled to make a second statement telling the truth of the story.' It is not a pleasant tale:

I was always guarded, someone watched me when I was sleeping, someone came with me to the toilet . . . The men told me I would be staying there as long as it took to 'deprogramme' me. They told me many examples of other members of religious societies who had been deprogrammed. Some stories were horrific.'

The final day was the worst.

'The fourth day they were becoming more and more heavy, I was becoming also weaker physically because of lack of food and exercise. I decided to try to pretend to the men that I agreed with whatever they said but could not continue because it made me feel sick, so I started screaming, smashed a window to try and escape, but they pulled me back and threw me on the bed. I was becoming hysterical, I ran downstairs (they ran after me), and tried to get out of the door, but they pulled me back again (my mother and sisters helped too) and threw me on the floor. I went upstairs again to take refuge in my bed, blocking my fingers in my ears and chanting, but they pulled off the bed clothes, held my hands on the bed and sat on me to stop me from moving. A few minutes later he got off me and I made a dash for the bedroom door, they pulled me back again and threw me on the bed, this happened two or three times. I was still screaming. They said that if I didn't 'behave myself' they would cut my hair off, take my clothes off and put me in the corner of the room. I was terrified. After that I just continued to scream, they started to undo my buttons (four buttons) on my blouse, but my mother was coming upstairs so they stopped.

Because her distress was so great her mother gave up the deprogramming and sent Miss Bradfield home. But her appalling treatment would eventually bring some good. In June 1984 she swore an affidavit reaffirming that John Mathewson had kidnapped her, and identifying him on a photograph which showed him in company with Richard Cottrell.

The association of Mr Cottrell with a known deprogrammer caused uproar. On 9 June 1984, the National Council of Hindu

Temples (UK), issued a press release which included Miss Bradfield's affidavit and noted that:

> It was brought to the attention of the National Council of Hindu Temples by the Bristol Hindu Temple representatives that Mr Cottrell (Euro MP for Bristol) appeared on national breakfast time television (TV-AM) on Monday 21st May 1984 with an ex-Hare Krishna member named John Mathewson. The National Council of Hindu Temples was greatly disturbed to see that Mr Cottrell was encouraging and accepting the support of Mr Mathewson, who has been positively identified by a young Hindu girl, Bernadette Bradfield, . . . as one of two men responsible for kidnapping and illegally detaining her for the purpose of forcibly attempting to make her reject her Hindu faith.

The inherent hostility of the Cottrell campaign to non-Christian faiths as well as to cults was now clear, and this played no small part in the ultimate failure of the campaign.

But deprogramming continues. In September 1991 the twenty-eight-year-old Viscount Reidhaven, son of the Earl of Seafield, was 'rescued' from the Naqshband sect of Sufism and deprogrammed at a cottage on the remote Knoydart peninsula in the Scottish highlands. His guru, Muhammed Ali, had allegedly been taking large sums of money from the Viscount – a common complaint against cult leaders and one that is all too often justified. It does not, however, justify abduction.

Nor is kidnapping and deprogramming confined to Christians. As a consequence of a continuing and aggressive campaign of proselytizing by the American evangelical group, Jews for Jesus, which seeks to convert Orthodox Jews to Christianity, a violent reaction has been set off. This has taken concrete form in *Operation Judaism* – a movement to combat the work of Jews for Jesus, but which unjustly claims that 'Jews are a prime target' for the 'Decade of Evangelism' promoted by all the mainstream British Churches. *Operation Judaism* aims to 'rescue' Jewish converts to Christianity, and was responsible, in November 1990, for the 'kidnapping' of two Jews who were due to be baptized as Christians – an action dismally reminiscent of the doings of the 'deprogrammers'. Rabbi Shmuel Arkush, who founded *Operation Judaism*, has also alleged (without giving confirmatory details) that conversion tactics have led to at least one Jewish suicide. (*The Independent on Sunday*, 16 December 1990.) More recently Mr Arkush has attacked the Church of England because of the work of the Churches Ministry among the Jews, while Judge Israel Finestein, president of the Board of Deputies of British Jews and by no means an extremist, urged his fellow Jews to combat the 'pernicious work' of the missionaries. (*The Independent*, 17 February 1992.)

There are also stories of Jewish violence against missionaries to the Jews; these, too, are largely impossible to confirm, but they are symptomatic of the anger and intolerance that results from fundamentalists of one faith being pitted against those of another. And inter-faith understanding is also strained by growing Islamic intolerance in Britain, exemplified especially by support given to the *fatwa* against Salman Rushdie. Nor will that intolerance be lessened by some aspects of the Anglican 'Decade of Evangelism' – such as statements by the Right Reverend Michael Marshall, that 'the call to win Islam for Christ is on the agenda.' Worse than this was the daubing of an East End London mosque with the slogan 'Jesus has died and is risen'. (Letter from the Reverend Kenneth Leech in *The Independent*, 31 December 1991.)

Such insensitive vandalism reflects the attitudes of the extreme wing of the evangelical movement. At the very edge is the Jesus Army, the aggressively evangelizing wing of the Jesus Fellowship Church, founded by a Baptist pastor, Noel Stanton. The church, which has some 1600 members, owns sixty community houses and a string of businesses – from farming to car repairs – and gains some of its recruits from the homeless, who are drawn into it as much by the prospect of food and accommodation as by its Christian message. Indoctrination follows, as does work for the Church's farms and businesses. Its form of evangelizing is so aggressive and extreme that it has been expelled from the Evangelical Alliance. It has all the hallmarks of a cult and thus should merit the condemnation of fundamentalists. But it saves souls for an unthinking and uncaring version of Christianity – it will not be condemned.

Nor will the intolerance that led to a divorced father facing jail, because he wished to take his four-year-old daughter to

Jehovah's Witnesses meetings, be condemned. The father had defied a court order banning him from taking the child to Sunday afternoon meetings and from trying to teach her the beliefs of the sect. He argued that he was justified because Article 9 of the European Convention on Human Rights guarantees a person's freedom of religion and to 'manifest his religion or belief, in worship, teaching, practice, and observance.' The court felt otherwise and supported the mother's wish to bring up her child as a Roman Catholic. (*The Independent on Sunday*, 15 September 1991.)

But if fundamentalists justify this action because it obeys the secular authority, they must also accept the actions of social workers in the London borough of Southwark, who removed a nine-year-old boy from his foster parents because they were 'indoctrinating him with religious beliefs' and this meant that he was being 'emotionally abused' by them. In this case, however, the 'extreme beliefs' of the foster parents, Graham and Sallie Warner, were those of the evangelical Christian group, the Ichthus Fellowship (*The Sunday Times*, 27 October 1991). There is a certain grim satisfaction in seeing the intolerant having to swallow their own medicine, but it is the child who will suffer most from the secular bigotry of the social workers.

And there are other social workers who have played a significant role in the most pernicious of all fundamentalist campaigns: the creation, promotion and operation of the myth of Satanism.

EIGHT

Satan in Suburbia

It is a commonplace for fundamentalists that all roads in the realm of the New Age lead to Hell, and in that sense all who travel them are Satanists. But even the most undisciplined of writers in this field recognize something that can be separated out and given the specific label of 'Satanism': the active worship of an evil principle as somehow 'good' with the parallel idea that the Christian God is the true evil being and that Christian morality must therefore be inverted.

The lurid, baroque visions that accompany the term today are, however, of modern origin, deriving from the attitudes and writings of the nineteenth-century French decadents, and from the curious occult groups with which they were associated. The standard picture of depraved rituals involving unfrocked priests, perversions and the degradation of everything that is sacred to the Christian, derives from J.K. Huysmans' novel *La Bas* the characters of which are based on contemporary occultists such as the Abbé Boullan, although they would have deplored the practices attributed to them. *La Bas* also stimulated the fertile imagination of Leo Taxil (*see* p.121 above) whose lurid tales of Luciferian Freemasons and human sacrifice found an audience of willing believers within the Roman Catholic Church, many of whom continued to believe even when Taxil announced that the whole affair began and ended in his own head.

Upon this foundation were built the fictitious Satanism of the novelist Dennis Wheatley – who lumped it with ritual magic in *The Devil Rides Out*, and brought the ceremonies of the Golden Dawn into *To the Devil a Daughter* – and the writings of that historian of witchcraft, Montague Summers. Both men have provided an inexhaustible quarry for fundamentalist writers, but Summers wins greater applause for his forthright condemnations: 'England has repealed the laws against witchcraft. The Divine Law she cannot repeal. "Thou shalt not suffer a Witch to live".' He also claims that human sacrifice is 'not unknown among the devil-worshippers today in London; in Brighton and Birmingham; in Oxford and Cambridge; in Edinburgh and Glasgow, and in a hundred cities more of the British Isles'. (M. Summers, *Witchcraft and Black Magic*, 1945, p.223.) We shall find disturbing echoes of his bloodthirsty fantasies, even at the present day.

But does it really exist today? Are there Satanists among us? There are numerous groups whose members are regularly labelled 'Satanists', but whether they merit the term in any meaningful sense is another matter. Some of them certainly do not. Publicity seeking, self-professed 'Satanists' such as Anton Sandor LaVey, whose 'First Church of Satan' was founded at San Francisco in 1966 are merely outrageous showmen. La Vey's 'Church' exists simply to invert traditional Christian sexual morality and to provide a specious justification for the antics of affluent and hedonistic Californians; it claims over one million members world-wide but this is a grossly inflated figure. Common-sense should be enough for the observer to see this 'Church' as the silly charade that it is – but fundamentalists still choose to believe that LaVey is somehow linked to an international satanic conspiracy and to hold up his ridiculous *Satanic Bible* (1969) as proof that organized Satanism is at work.

Others, like the the ex-Scientologist Robert Sylvester de Grimstone Moore, are more unpleasant. De Grimstone founded his 'Process Church of the Final Judgement' at London in 1964. Starting life as an odd form of psychotherapy, it developed into a semi-religious cult and eventually into a full-blown 'Church', proclaiming that Satan and Christ are equally present in everyone and that one ought to love Satan as an example of loving one's enemies. In practice it was no more than yet another bizarre sect offering curious rituals, a quite lunatic theology, and hostile pronouncements against orthodox Christianity.

For a time the Process Church harboured one really evil member, Charles Manson, whose hippy commune (The Family) accepted him as a satanic Jesus Christ, and in 1969 helped him to carry out a series of sadistic murders, for which crimes he is still imprisoned. Manson is typical of psychopaths who link occult fantasies with their violent criminal activities, but he is not a Satanist. Other criminals have claimed to be: Richard Ramirez, the 'Night Stalker' who in 1989 was found guilty of fourteen murders in the USA, clearly believed that he was a Satanist. Many other similar instances could be cited, but a catalogue of horrors will serve no purpose; what must be stressed, however, is that in no recorded case of what has been called 'satanic crime' is there evidence of organized ritual activity. Contrary to the beliefs of fundamentalist and other writers on the subject, these crimes are not the work of Satanists, but of individual psychopaths (and occasionally groups) who seize upon occult symbols and language simply because they are there. If they were not they would merely hang their murders on a different peg.

And beside the showmen and the criminals are the magicians – specifically there is Aleister Crowley, a disturbed rather than a disturbing man, whose pretentious rituals and juvenile black humour are treated with deadly seriousness both by credulous fundamentalists and by secular authors who ought to know better. Crowley has always received a bad press, and with some justice, but he was essentially a child of the 1890s whose 'wickedness' was that of decadence: sexual perversion and a childish desire to shock the establishment. To the fundamentalist, however, he has come to represent Satanism at its worst: a child-sacrificing monster, corrupting all around him. But his petty blasphemies were human sin, not the utter chilling evil of Hitler or Stalin.

At which point it will be as well to sweep away the nonsensical stories of Crowley's supposed human sacrifices. They are used as proof of a tradition of child abuse and child murder within Satanism, but they have no foundation. In his book *Magick in Theory and Practice* Crowley refers to 'a male child of perfect innocence and high intelligence' as the most 'satisfactory and suitable victim' for the 'Bloody Sacrifice'. He notes also that: 'It appears from the Magical Records of Frater Perdurabo [i.e. Crowley] that he made this particular sacrifice on an average about 150 times every year between 1912 and 1928'. (Aleister Crowley, *Magick*, edited by J. Symonds and K. Grant 1973, p.219). But he is not referring to human sacrifice. If one reads his diaries, which promoters of the satanic myth clearly do not, then the meaning becomes plain: Crowley is referring to sex acts, most commonly to masturbation. His practices may be distasteful and revolting, but they do not constitute murder.

The myth-makers, however, will have none of it. For Tim Tate, 'The text is too specific to allow it to be read symbolically' (T. Tate, *Children for the Devil: Ritual Abuse and Satanic Crime*, 1991, p.101); while David Hallam, a former employee of the National Children's Home, led a successful campaign to have the book withdrawn by the publishers, Penguin. The company commented:

> While disliking any acts of censorship, we at Penguin feel that in certain circumstances the book can be used as a force for harm, and therefore have decided to withdraw it. (Andrew Boyd, *Blasphemous Rumours* 1991, p.126.)

The story is too important a weapon for fundamentalists for them to drop it because of the small matter of intellectual honesty.

Where, then, are the real Satanists? A survey of his customers by Chris Bray of 'The Sorcerer's Apprentice' shop at Leeds led to extravagant claims that 'a quarter of a million Britons would describe themselves as witches or pagans. Of these, four per cent apparently regard themselves as Satanists. If Mr Bray is anywhere near the mark, that would extrapolate to some 10,000 *professing* Satanists in the UK.' (A. Boyd, *Blasphemous Rumours*, 1991, p.161) In fact it would do nothing of the sort, for the original sample was of little more than 1,000 individuals drawn from a group highly sympathetic to the occult. Of these, just forty-one professed to be practising Satanists.

Such people should be approached more in sorrow than in anger. From their bizarre publications – which have minimal circulation – they exhibit clear signs of paranoid delusion and other forms of psychological disturbance; they may be perceived as either pathetic or pretentious, but they are not the advance guard of Satan's army. Nor are the supposed escapees from Satan's clutches a sign of active Satanism, but this latter group has an infinitely greater capacity to cause unwarranted distress to the public and to bring persecution upon the innocent.

If we ignore the ex-witch John Todd, the first escapee was Doreen Irvine (*see* pp.44–5 above), but she professed to be a 'black witch' rather than a Satanist, thus perpetuating the confusion between witchcraft and Satanism – much to the fury of modern self-styled witches, who are pagans indeed but who have no leanings towards deliberate evil.

Her tales have also been surpassed by those of a more recent ex-Satanist, Audrey Harper, who recounts her evildoing with remarkable gusto in her book, *Dance with the Devil* (1990). This book feeds the fires of fantasy and merits close examination.

Dance with the Devil opens with a foreword by Geoffrey Dickens, the Conservative MP for Littleborough and Saddleworth who has long sought to persuade Parliament to legislate against the occult. It is, he says:

> . . . one of the most important books on the evils of devil worship published for many years. Sad to report, Audrey's story is not untypical, because the fear of the devil put into victims makes them too terrified to tell and break away. Audrey Harper has bravely escaped from the terrors of Satanism and black witchcraft. I am delighted that, with the support of Christ, Audrey Harper has found the strength to tell her story through the pen of Harry Pugh.' (A. Harper, *Dance with the Devil*, 1990, p.9)

Mr Dickens undoubtedly believes that Audrey Harper, the co-author and subject of the book, is telling the unvarnished truth. Two years before he had appeared on Central TV's *Weekend* programme, in company with Miss Harper, to make the point with dramatic effect. During the programme he had asked her: 'Audrey, to your knowledge, is child sacrifice going on?' to which she replied, 'To my knowledge, yes' (p.206).

But what is her story? As with Doreen Irvine whose tale is so similar in many ways, Audrey Harper supposedly entered

Satanism by way of prostitution and drug addiction, being initiated on 31 October 1961, in a purpose-built temple adjoining a large house at Virginia Water in Surrey. There the similarity ends – and clearly the two witches never met, for the many hundreds of orgiastic 'black witches' of Miss Irvine's experience do not match Miss Harper's more select but even more evil band of Satanists. The Harper initiation was a much nastier affair, much more akin to the satanic sacrificial ceremony of the film version of *The Devil Rides Out* for it incorporated human sacrifice: a nine day old baby in place of Miss Irvine's cockerel. There was also ritualized sex and the signing of a pact in blood, although this one read 'I am no longer my own. Satan is my master. I live to serve him only.' The life of devil-worship that followed was much the same for Audrey Harper as it was for Doreen Irvine: an endless round of drugs, perverted sex, desecration of churches, and supernatural wonders. But there was one extra ingredient: the sexual abuse of children. This, says Miss Harper, 'was the part that sickened me most of all' but she yet gives several pages of revolting detail (presumably to reinforce the horror felt by 'Christian' readers) and adds one highly original detail.

She was, or claims to have been, a 'brood mare': a woman selected to produce babies for the purpose of sacrificing them to Satan (a topic, it might be added, on which Maureen Davies dwells with relish in her audio-tape *Satanic Ritual Abuse*, giving a detailed analysis of the varied uses – murder and cannibalism – to which foetuses and unregistered full-term babies are put); and her anxiety for her unborn child is what led her eventually to escape from her 'coven'. There are, even so, far too many incongruities, inconsistencies and sheer impossibilities in her story for it to be reliable and correct. She finally revealed her tale of child-murder and abuse in 1986, after her 'conversion', although 'after twenty-five years my memory was hazy' and she was unable to take the police to the house at Virginia Water, or to give them 'names and addresses, dates, phone numbers and car registrations' – even though the date of her initiation and all the revolting details of her satanic activities were crystal clear in her mind. What one concludes from her story (whether in her book, or from the videotapes *Doorway to Danger* and *Devil Worship*) depends on one's viewpoint; to the fundamentalists it is conclusive proof from a fervent convert that satanic wickedness flourishes, while to the rational observer it is yet one more instance of the fantasies of fundamentalist obsessions.

The 'brood mare' story may or may not have originated with Audrey Harper, but elsewhere she claims to have met others than herself:

> I'm talking to one woman who was made pregnant four times and had to have an abortion all four times so that the foetus could be sacrificed. The fourth time she had to do the killing . . . [Another girl] . . . had to kill her own baby . . . [but despite such evil] . . . I won't let the police or the media talk to my girls because they don't believe them and it leaves them even worse off. (*The Independent*, 2 October 1990)

She does leave the door to proof slightly ajar – 'The time will come when the evidence will be there' – but for the objective observer an inevitable scepticism sets in.

But not for the fundamentalist. The active presence of Satan and his demons in the world is a necessary part of his creed, and to prop up that part he must seek out the signs of Satan. They are to be found in every instance of occultism, in every manifestation of the New Age, and in every New Religious Movement and every apostasy from the Church. But the public is blind to these signs and must be given something that cannot be ignored. If that something produces a powerful emotional response, so much the better. And nothing is more emotive or so guaranteed to arouse public anger as violence done to children, especially when such violence is coupled with Satanism.

The supposed link between Satanism and child sacrifice is of long standing: it featured in the trial of the renegade Abbé Guibourg in the seventeenth century. But child abuse, specifically sexual abuse, is a new feature in stories of Satanism. That child abuse exists cannot be denied, and the dedication of those who seek to rescue children from abuse and to heal their damaged psyches cannot be praised too highly. But there are others whose enthusiasm is tinged with credulity and turns to fanaticism; whose critical judgement vanishes when faced with tales of devil-worship, and who end by doing harm where they sought to do good.

Many hysterical tales are clearly nonsensical – no reasonable person can believe that 4,000 children a year are being sacrificed in Britain and that 'three children, aged 8, 10 and 11, had been crucified upside down and forced into sex acts at a ritual last April for Satan's birthday' (Dianne Core of Childwatch, quoted in *The New Federalist*, 15 November, 1988) – but others are within the bounds of credibility and they have led to criminal prosecutions that have damaged and destroyed the lives of the accused, who are in almost every case wholly innocent.

Ritual abuse has been defined as 'abuse that occurs in a context linked to some symbols or group activity that have a religious, magical or supernatural connotation, and where the invocation of these symbols or activities, repeated over time, is used to frighten and intimidate the children'. (T. Tate, *Children for the Devil*, 1991, p.3, quoting Finkelhor *et al*, *Nursery Crimes – Child Abuse in Day Care*, 1988.) It does not necessarily involve supposed Satanism, but in practice the satanic connection is always emphasised.

Stories of the sexual abuse of children in the context of satanic rituals began with the published memoirs of alleged 'adult survivors' of such abuse. These were invariably women whose current psychological disturbance was traced back to sexual abuse at any early age, the memory of which had been suppressed and could be brought out only by psychotherapy and hypnotherapy. As an aside it is worthy of note that the use of hypnosis in these cases has not been condemned by fundamentalist authors who perceive it as a demonic practice in other circumstances.

The first recorded 'adult survivor' was a Canadian woman, Michelle Smith, the author – with her therapist and later husband, Lawrence Pazder – of *Michelle Remembers* (1980), a book portrayed as 'The true story of a year-long contest between innocence and evil.' According to Mrs Smith, she was brought to Satanism at the age of five by her own mother. Her sufferings included sexual abuse, the desecration of graveyards, animal mutilation and the regular ritual sacrifice of human babies; but they did not continue beyond

early childhood, the memories were suppressed and she grew
to normal adulthood in Victoria, British Columbia.

The psychotherapy that revealed these horrors followed her
distress after a miscarriage, and aided by the active spiritual
support of local Roman Catholic clergy (she was exorcized
by the Bishop of Victoria), resulted in her coming to terms
with her terrible suppressed memories. Except that they
were not suppressed, being nothing more than subconscious
inventions.

The real childhood of Michelle Smith was spent with a
kind mother who took her regularly to church; in the words
of her father, Jack Proby: 'There never was a woman on this
earth who worked harder for her daughters. There was no
hanky-panky or devil worshipping'. (Denna Allen and Janet
Midwinter, 'The Debunking of a Myth', in *The Mail on Sunday*,
30 September 1990.) Neighbours also 'dismissed the book as
crazy' but the damage was done: 'Ritual Abuse' (the term
was coined by Dr Pazder) has entered the fundamentalist
vocabulary, and Michelle Smith is regularly paraded before
the public as a prime example of a victim of Satanism.

What is most shameful is that the proponents of the 'satanic
abuse' myth are highly selective when presenting evidence
from this and other cases to support their claims. Thus Tim
Tate states, in reference to Michelle Smith, that 'Pazder knew
by the end that his patient was not fabricating or fantasizing
the recollections. There was simply too much detail, too deeply
felt'. (T. Tate, *Children for the Devil*, p.48.) Andrew Boyd refers
to the criticisms of *Michelle Remembers*, but rejects them and
comments: 'If the account was a fabrication, contrived to
persuade an audience of both its credibility and authenticity,
then it has missed a good many tricks, because there are too
many odd, bizarre and apparently silly details which beggar
belief.' (Andrew Boyd, *Blasphemous Rumours*, p.272.)

But neither author refers to those parts of the narrative
that require the reader to believe in the physical presence
of a fire-breathing Satan, chanting endless doggerel verse
and giving visions of a literal Hell during an eighty-two-
day ceremony that involved dozens of attendants bringing
murdered infants as the bread and wine of a Black Mass.
There are sixty pages of this arrant nonsense in the book

(pp. 225–284), reminiscent of both Dennis Wheatley's fiction and the inventions of Leo Taxil – but they are never quoted as they completely undermine its credibility from within.

Another 'survivor' soon appeared, and one whose story was more appealing to fundamentalist ears. Michelle Smith was a Roman Catholic and her final deliverance was brought about by Catholic exorcism, something that could not find favour with evangelical Protestants. Lauren Stratford (the pen-name of Laurel Rose Wilson) was altogether more respectable. Her sensational book *Satan's Underground* (1988) has sold 100,000 copies – almost all in fundamentalist circles.

It tells of a life of degradation and brutality; of repeated sexual abuse as a child; of an adult life spent drifting downwards through prostitution and drugs to Satanism. As a participant in satanic rituals (she denies having been a true Satanist) Lauren Stratford was again sexually abused and took part in the sacrifice of human infants, including her own son Joey. Eventually she escaped from the Satanists, went through a long period of mental illness, was spiritually healed and 'born again'. Her book followed, and with it her work as a counsellor of victims of ritual abuse.

The trouble with her story of childhood abuse and later Satanism is that it has been shown to be untrue. A detailed investigation into her story was carried out by three evangelical Christians, Gretchen and Bob Passantino and Jon Trott.[1] From this investigation a picture emerges of a confused and emotionally disturbed adult who had passed through an equally disturbed adolescence with continual difficulties over personal relationships, but at no time was there any hint of sexual abuse – in childhood or later. Nor was she involved at any time with either drugs or prostitution. Her stories of Satanism did not emerge until 1985 and they varied widely from confidante to confidante, but every story proved to be untrue. When she was taken up by prominent fundamentalists (Johanna Michaelson and Hal Lindsey) who did not know her background, her fantasies were believed – but they were unable subsequently to prove *any* of Lauren's claims. What is certain is that Lauren Stratford was never sexually abused; never had children; lied about her connection with cases of ritual abuse; and was never involved with Satanism.

And what is most disturbing about her story is its effect upon trusting innocents; as her critics say:

> *Satan's Underground* has become the basis, the foundation, for Lauren Stratford's authority as an expert on ritualistic abuse and as a counselor of other victims. Because the story is not true the foundation is illusory, and her expertise and counseling qualifications are nonexistent.

But her book has helped to propagate the larger myth.

As a direct consequence of the sensational tales of 'adult survivors', fears began to spread of organized Satanism corrupting young children at kindergartens. The first case of 'ritual' or 'satanic' abuse involving children arose at Manhattan Beach near Los Angeles in 1983, where children at the McMartin pre-school Day Care Centre were allegedly subjected to systematic sexual abuse by staff. Subsequent court cases exonerated the defendants, who had been arraigned on 208 counts of child sexual molestation, but tales of 'Satanism' continued to circulate and eventually other local residents were also accused. After seven years, every charge was dismissed, but the finger of suspicion is still pointed at the accused and the smears continue: 'few investigators would have doubted that the children had been molested sexually'. (Carl Raschke, *Painted Black*, 1990, p.65.) And the affair led some social workers to believe that 'organised satanic cults [are] using day-care centres to gain access to children'. (Valerie Sinason, 'Talk of the Devil' in *The Weekend Guardian*, 3 November 1990.)

A rash of accusations of 'satanic ritual abuse' followed the McMartin case, leading to such active persecution as that suffered by Jill Simpson in Pennsylvania. What they have in common is that none of them has been sustained in court. There have indeed been, as there doubtless always will be, instances of the sexual abuse of children, both by relatives and by those who nominally care for children, but there has not yet been a single proven case of the physical, sexual or emotional abuse of children in the context of Satanism, or of any other magical or occult practice.

The absence of proof is not, however, sufficient to stop the 'satanic ritual abuse' bandwagon. In Britain it has moved from Nottingham, to Rochdale, to the Orkney Islands, and to Epping Forest. The assorted 'experts' who follow it around are adept at seeking out and finding Satanists and examples of their child abuse, but they have signally failed to translate their findings into successful prosecutions. Not, however, for the want of trying.

In February 1989 the first major case of alleged 'ritual' or 'Satanic' abuse in Britain was brought to trial at Nottingham. It was an appalling case in which a total of twenty-five children had been subjected to sexual abuse within their deprived and degenerate extended family; at the trial nine adults – of whom eight were family members – pleaded guilty and were imprisoned for incest and other crimes. There the matter would have rested were it not that social workers involved in the case became perplexed and disturbed by some of the stories told by the children. They spoke of being taken to tunnels in a cemetery, of being ritually mutilated, and of animal and human sacrifice – in addition to the horrors of sexual abuse (all tales with parallels in the story of Michelle Smith); they also implicated adults who were not members of their family. All of these allegations were subsequently thoroughly investigated by the police, who concluded that there was no corroborative evidence and dismissed the 'satanic' elements out of hand.

Against this was the conviction of the social workers concerned that the children *were* telling the truth and they put their case in a television programme (*Dispatches* on Channel 4) on 3 October 1990. 'Evidence' was shown on the programme; social workers and foster parents were interviewed, and a frightening case was built up. But did it stand up to objective analysis? It did not. The police provided counter explanations for each 'satanic' claim – the tunnels under the graveyard had long since been searched and nothing found; the claims that sacrificed bodies had been buried in existing graves were dismissed because there was nothing to show that any graves had been disturbed – and there was a sound explanation of how the children's stories originated:

> The children were given toys to symbolize good and bad during play therapy with social workers from the NSPCC. These included witches' costumes, monsters and snakes. The children began to talk of these items only after this play therapy, and foster parents then wrote about them in diaries recording everything the children said. (Report by Rosie Waterhouse in *The Independent*, 4 November 1990.)

And by this time both social workers and foster parents had acquired from America lists of supposed 'indicators' of 'satanic abuse'.

The social workers also faced the anger of the Chief Constable of Nottinghamshire, Dan Crompton, who was furious that 'a team of social workers should continue to make claims that exhaustive investigations by police and other social workers have been unable to corroborate with hard evidence.' (*The Independent on Sunday*, 7 October 1990.) Also, adult witnesses to Satanism and sacrifice in the case were 'found to be lying in every respect that could actually be checked.' This, however, was not the end of the matter. The social workers countered by arguing that 'we were not given the "indicators" until we'd already heard the children's stories' and by claiming that 'senior police officers then tried to intimidate social workers and threatened to discredit us if we continued to ask for further investigation' [into the involvement of other adults outside the family concerned]. (Judith Dawson 'Vortex of Evil' in *New Statesman and Society*, 5 October 1990.)

But how did a knowledge of 'satanic ritual abuse' come to Britain? All the indications are that it came from the USA but precisely how it came is not known. What is certain, however, is that the drive for a general acceptance of widespread Satanism and 'satanic ritual abuse' was spearheaded by Maureen Davies and the Reachout Trust, with the active support of members of the Evangelical Alliance (Clive Calver, the Alliance's General Director, is on the Council of Reference of the Reachout Trust and can be presumed to endorse their pronouncements), and such clerical enthusiasts for spiritual warfare as the Reverend Kevin Logan of Great Harwood in

Lancashire. Mrs Davies's views have been disseminated by way of audio-tapes of her lectures, distributed by the Reachout Trust, television appearances, and reports and interviews in the national press. According to some of these, her influence is considerable, as she 'is consulted by police officers and social workers, and has lectured at police training colleges and to church groups'; while 'her belief in the existence of Satanism and her determination to stamp out the evil is unshakeable'. (*Wales on Sunday*, 23 September 1990.)

She also claimed that: 'The Reachout Trust is aware of thirty satanic ritual abuse rings operating in Britain, many of which have come to light in the last twelve months' (*Western Mail*, 14 August 1989). Evidence to substantiate her claim was not forthcoming, although in June 1990 the Reachout Trust did issue a four-page dossier of evidence giving 'definitive proof' of the reality of satanic crime and ritual abuse. This listed thirty-one cases, but none of them stood up to critical analysis. (*Bad News Journal*, no.15, 1990.)

Warnings of the spread of Satanism also came to Britain with Miss Sandi Gallant (now Mrs Bargioni), a Police Intelligence Officer with the San Francisco Police Department, who gave lectures early in 1988 in which she spoke of the increase in animal and human sacrifice in the USA with the suggestion that it could also happen here. She provided both guidelines for investigating ritual abuse and a list of 'case problems' that investigators might face. The most startling of these is the problem arising when 'no evidence is found at alleged crime scenes to substantiate statements made by the victims.' This has a parallel in an American report of 1988:

> Pennsylvania State Trooper Robert Scutta has also been studying 'ritualistic crime' . . . Scutta and others well versed in ritualistic crime know that the most high-level, well-organized groups practice sophisticated surveillance against discovery by the police, and never leave evidence of their rites or sacrifices. Therefore, police departments often have no clue as to their existence . . . (File 18 Newsletter. December 1988, quoting from an article on 'Satanic Crime' in the *Sunday News* of Lancaster, PA)

In other words, these crimes are alleged to happen but there is no evidence that they have happened. Such is the language of myth-makers.

Also in 1988 social workers in Kent sought advice about a child in their care – only to learn from an American 'expert', Pamela Klein, that it was a classic case of 'satanic abuse'. Miss Klein supplied them with a list of 'satanic indicators' which had been drawn up by Pamela Hudson, a psychiatric social worker and child therapist of Mendocino in California. The list – which is not for the squeamish – was then circulated to a number of social workers throughout the country, including those investigating the Nottingham case. By 1989 the idea of satanic abuse was firmly implanted in both the fundamentalist mind and that of secular therapists and social workers.

Not all cases were brought to court; for many adult 'survivors' it was neither feasible nor desirable, although in some instances the treatment that they did receive was an even more undesirable course of action. The story of Caroline Marchant is a case in point.

Caroline Marchant professed to be a victim of satanic abuse and to have been involved in child sacrifice – a story promoted posthumously in the press (the *Sunday Mirror* ran the story in March 1990 under the headline 'I sacrificed my babies to Satan'). Her story, however, was utterly untrue; her life paralleled that of Lauren Stratford – an emotionally disturbed childhood, difficulty with relationships, and a constant confusion of reality and fantasy. Many of the 'satanic' elements in her story seem to have been derived from the work of Doreen Irvine (who counselled Miss Marchant in 1987 at the Zion Christian Temple at Yate, near Bristol. (*The Independent on Sunday Review*, 30 December 1990.)[2] What she needed most was psychiatric help, whereas what she received was spiritual counselling by fundamentalists who saw demons rather than a disturbed mind. In February 1990, while in the care of the Reverend Kevin Logan, Caroline Marchant committed suicide.

Cases that have led to legal action have not yet resulted in any deaths, but they have brought untold misery to the innocent, both children and adults. In the two episodes that follow, all the satanic myths propagated by ignorance are prominent. The more recent case involved allegations of sexual abuse, human sacrifice and cannibalism.

At an Old Bailey court in November 1991, two young sisters (then aged ten and fourteen) alleged that they had been forced to take part in the ritual killing and eating of babies in Epping Forest, and that they were sexually abused in the course of devil-worshipping ceremonies. These horrifying charges were brought against their parents, godparents and a family friend. But after a week of evidence so sickening that 'no newspaper can bring itself to publish the full details', the case collapsed. The younger girl stated that although her evidence of ill-treatment was true she 'was not sure whether she had imagined the killings or not.' The prosecuting counsel offered no further evidence and admitted that he 'could no longer rely' on the younger child's evidence. As a consequence of what the judge termed 'so uncertain, inconsistent and improbable' evidence, the accused were all acquitted.

But being found innocent could not remove the injustice, or the suffering caused by a trial that should never have taken place. For the godparents, Rosemary Ridewood and Sonny Gibbard, both of whom are devout Christians, the affair had been a nightmare. 'It was,' said Mrs Ridewood, 'as if somebody had filled a bucket from a cesspit and poured it all over me.' The children's mother said: 'The girls made it all up. They learned about the satanic things in horror films and videos,' while their father commented: 'We have lost our homes, our jobs and been to prison. They believed the word of children and never even questioned it.' (*The Observer*, 17 November 1991; *The Daily Mail*, 20 November 1991; *The Sunday Telegraph*, 24 November 1991.) Ironically, it was a film (*Do You Know the Muffin Man*) about satanic rituals at a day-care centre that led to Jill Simpson being accused of satanic abuse; but it was seen by the parents and not by the children.

The children in the Epping case had themselves gone through a cruel and damaging farce that could scar them emotionally for life. And yet both fundamentalist myth-makers and their secular allies still raise the cry of 'Believe the children' – first used as a slogan in the McMartin case. In March 1991 Christopher Brown, director of the NSPCC, referred to children's allegations of ritual abuse and stated that 'the NSPCC would be failing in its duty if it did not listen to these children.' This view was supported by Tim Tate, who insisted that: 'Academic and clinical studies show that children have highly accurate recall of events in which they have been involved.' (T.Tate, *Children for the Devil*, p.231.)

Stories by children also led to accusations of satanic abuse in the Orkney Islands. In February 1991 nine children from four families were seized from their parents in dawn raids, by police and social workers, on the island of South Ronaldsay. The children were taken to foster homes on the Scottish mainland where they remained for five weeks while their parents stood accused of sexual abuse in the course of satanic rituals conducted by the island's Church of Scotland minister, the Reverend Morris McKenzie.

The social workers had believed allegations of ritualistic abuse made by three disturbed children who had previously been taken into care after their father had been imprisoned for sexually abusing them. The minister and members of other families on the island had tried to help the mother and her remaining children, and it was this practical Christian charity that had led to accusations of Satanism. But the stories of the satanic rituals and alleged abuse were so inconsistent that on 3 April the Sheriff of Orkney, David Kelbie, dismissed the case as 'fatally flawed'. But the Orkney Social Services department persisted in their attempts to prosecute until June when the case was finally dropped even though an appeal against the first dismissal had succeeded. A judicial inquiry was set up which is expected to report at the end of 1992.

What this outline does not convey is the suffering and despair of both the children and their parents. The children had been denied letters from their parents as well as their own toys and personal possessions. They were questioned in a sickening, prurient manner which disgusted them and when they finally returned to their parents they were angry, hurt and bitter. The parents were equally embittered. Their characters had been smeared and the smear, utterly unjust though it is, remains. But their greatest anger concerned their children. One mother said simply, 'My children have been mentally and sexually assaulted. Their persecutors were not Satanists, however, but the NSPCC, the social workers and the police. (*The Observer* and *The Sunday Times*, 7 April 1991.)

Another facet of this persecution was religious. It was made public by the Reverend Ian Cohen of Chalgrove, Oxford, who knows the family concerned. 'It is also further distressing,' he wrote, 'for the devoutly Quaker family of two boys, who have been separated since being taken into care (one to a foster home), to be told by Orkney Social Services that a Quaker boarding school is not an acceptable "place of safety". To have this added to a report by their mother that when being interviewed about her beliefs as a Quaker, she was asked whether or not it was strange to "sit in a circle" in "silence".' (Letter to *Church Times*, 28 March 1991.)

Evidently only witches and Satanists are expected to behave in such a way.

Fear and ignorance lie behind all these cases, but there are other prejudices too. Andrew Boyd recites a catalogue of anti-masonic sentiments by carers involved in ritual abuse cases, and states that 'a masonic connection has been mentioned by many carers. They have been told of it by their clients, and some say they have encountered it for themselves, where strings have been pulled to close a masonic net over an investigation or prosecution.' And there is more. He quotes accounts from a variety of professionals concerned with 'satanic abuse' and sums up their comments by stating that, 'criminal Satanism would appear to be a sexist, class-ridden institution, where men with power and influence exert absolute authority over women and children and use working men as their minions'. (Andrew Boyd, *Blasphemous Rumours*, pp.164 and 167.)

To anti-Masonry is added the politics of envy, and all this poisonous venom continues to flow into the consciousness of the public adding extra dimensions to a baseless myth. Those who suffer are those who are supposedly being saved. Their plight is encapsulated in the words of the American child psychiatrist, Richard Gardner:

> Children embroiled in false sex abuse allegations are victims in another sense. They are the victims of the parade of parents, 'validators', 'therapists', prosecutors, and other legal and mental health professionals who use them to serve their own ends. Our sympathies must also go out to these children as well as the adult victims of false sex abuse allegations. (R. Gardner, *Sex Abuse Hysteria, Salem Witch Trials Revisited*, 1991, p.139.)

Who then is really doing the devil's work? And more importantly, how can they be stopped?

NOTES TO CHAPTER EIGHT

1. A full report is published in the Christian magazine, *Cornerstone*, vol. 18, no. 90.
2. The case was analysed by David Hebditch and Nick Anning.

NINE

Fighting for Freedom

There are many who will argue that there is no need to fight against fundamentalism and its fears and fantasies, that it is no more than 'a tale told by an idiot, full of sound and fury, signifying nothing.' But this is a short sighted view. The champions of 'satanic abuse' may have been embarrassed; televangelists may be discomfited; and the New Christian Right may have been dissipated as a political force, but they are still there, awaiting their time. They have not gone away and they will not go away, because they are not concerned simply with the next case or the next election. Their concern is with eternity and they will never cease from returning to the fray.

The public has a short memory, and the follies and failures of fundamentalists and those whom they inspire are soon forgotten. If their steady erosion of civil liberties – of freedoms of expression, belief and worship – is to be halted they must be continually held in check. Their weapons are an unbending absolutist faith and a simplistic world-view that is reinforced by a widespread and wide-ranging ignorance. Such a faith gives them their strength, but in their ignorance lies their weakness.

Without exception, fundamentalist controversial works display an ignorance of the subjects they combat, whether these are other faiths, cults, alternative medicine, the New Age, or the 'occult'. By exposing the errors that result from this ignorance – and the deceit which, on occasion, feeds it – their arguments can be defeated. And then the question of motive can be examined.

Examples of such errors have been given throughout this book, and more could be given from every fundamentalist source that has been cited. This would serve little purpose, however, and it is enough that the reader is encouraged to read those sources himself and to correct and publicize the errors that he finds. It must be emphasized that the most important of such errors of fact are those that find their way into secular studies of 'alternative' faiths and practices and thus provide support for the negative constructions placed by fundamentalists upon such practices and beliefs. Tim Tate's *Children for the Devil*, for example, is littered with historical, literary and biographical errors that indicate too great a reliance on unsound sources and a strong leaning towards credulity.[1] Similarly Carl Raschke, the author of a recent study of Satanism, *Painted Black* (1990), serves up errors and old fables as truth – although as Director of the Institute for Humanities, and Professor of Religious Studies at the University of Denver, he ought to know better.

What is even more important is the exposure of deliberate deception. This rarely occurs in the work of fundamentalist propagandists, but they are often prone to accepting the claims of those who do deceive, such as John Todd and 'Leo Taxil'. The fictions of Leo Taxil were made known in 1897 when their author, Gabriel Jogand Pages, admitted that the whole affair of the satanic Palladium was a hoax, a fiction created by himself to embarrass the Roman Catholic Church. 'The Palladium exists no more', he said, 'I was the creator of it, and I have destroyed it. You have nothing more to fear from its sinister influence. The great enemy of Christian men and of the Catholic Church is dead.' (Rhodes, *The Satanic Mass*, p.195.)

But his stories are still believed in fundamentalist circles, and because of the sectarian hatred that they can generate it is desirable that the Taxil stories, and later lies founded upon them, are identified and shown to be false – however disastrous the consequences may be for those who have pinned their faith upon them. One instance of their occurrence is in the work of the 'Freed Mason', Ian Gordon.

In his book *The Cross and the Craft* (1989), Mr Gordon describes how, having left Freemasonry, he 'asked God to show me clearly why I had to renounce Freemasonry' (p.154) and so 'God led me to discover this irrefutable evidence that the Order which I loved more than any other had been presided over by, and received its instructions from a practising Luciferian' (p.160). The Luciferian, of course, is Albert Pike (*see* p.121 above) but the information about him was both erroneous and deliberately deceptive.

It is derived from the book *La Femme et l'enfant dans la Franc-Maconnerie universelle* (1894) by Mme A.C. de la Rive, which printed the text of a set of 'Instructions' allegedly issued by Pike to twenty-three Scottish Rite Supreme Councils throughout the world on 14 July 1889 (which date indicates a French rather than an American origin). According to this text 'Lucifer is God' and 'If Lucifer were not God would Adonay (The God of the Christians) whose deeds prove his cruelty, perfidy and hatred of man, barbarism and repulsion for science, would Adonay and his priests calumniate him?' – together with much more in similarly satanic vein. The problem for Mr Gordon, and for others with similar opinions, is that Pike issued no such instructions – no original, either in manuscript or in print has ever been produced – and they conflict with Pike's forthright opposition to using pagan names for God.

The 'Instructions' were a fiction, and other 'irrefutable evidence' to which his 'god' led Mr Gordon is similarly tainted. The whole farrago of nonsense concerning the Rosicrucian and Luciferian origins of Freemasonry is drawn indirectly from the works of Leo Taxil, and more immediately from *Occult Theocrasy* (1933), by Lady Queenborough. Because of the fraudulent nature of this 'irrefutable evidence', one is drawn to asking just which god led Mr Gordon to accept these lies as truth? The uncomfortable answer can only be that it was a god of lies, that is, Satan himself. How Mr Gordon accommodates this fact to his fundamentalist faith will be a matter for his own conscience.

John Todd poses a more difficult problem. The impact upon American fundamentalists of his fantastic stories of witchcraft, Druids and the Illuminati, and of his astounding claims about the occult involvement of American politicians and other prominent citizens, was immense. These stories and allegations also influenced the views of the more credulous fundamentalists in Britain, notably Maureen Davies and Dianne Core. They are also still being propagated through the 'Christian' comic-books of Jack Chick, one of which, *Spellbound*, begins with a clear statement about Todd: 'My deepest appreciation to John Todd, ex-Grand Druid Priest, for the authenticity of the occult information used in this story. Also to those others who came out of witchcraft and have verified this material.' That Todd's words are still widely presented as being true, despite his exposure by concerned evangelical Christians, is an indictment of fundamentalist integrity, and it is essential that the story of his downfall be made more widely known.

Todd's nemesis came in 1978 and 1979 when he began to make outrageous attacks upon prominent Christians (*see* p. 117 above). He maintained a continuing, if sporadic, involvement with witchcraft and occultism in general and alternated between Christian and occult commitment. His claims about the Illuminati became ever more absurd: 'John F. Kennedy was not really killed; I just came back from a visit with him on his yacht'; while he also alleged that he had 'witnessed the stabbing of a girl by Senator George McGovern in an act of sacrifice.' A detailed analysis of his life history and his claims about occultism appeared in February 1979 in the highly respected journal, *Christianity Today*, under the title of 'The Bewitching of the Churches: The Legends of John Todd'. The article poses the question: 'Is what John Todd is saying true?' and gives an unequivocal answer:

> No, it is not. Todd was not at the pinnacle of a witches' conspiracy for global conquest as he claims to have been. He has not launched key organizations in the Charismatic movement or the modern gospel music industry by signing a few checks for them from witch headquarters. He has not been to many of the places (like Duke University and Viet Nam) he says he has been. His memory is fitful. He cannot even seem to remember his right age from one reporter to the next. Important details of the story he tells change from town to town. (p. 12)

Todd's army medical records indicate – among other problems – severe personality disturbance, emotional instability, and difficulty in telling fantasy from reality. It is unfortunate that so many in his audiences emulated him in this last respect.

Other fundamentalist absurdities that pass for reality are born in the minds of assorted converts: ex-New Agers, ex-Freemasons, and ex-witches. Careful analysis of what they write will enable any objective reader to make a reasoned refutation of their claims. But why are such claims made?

Presumably they are intended to further the theological stance of their authors, and so it is only just to consider what motivates them to take that stance. Some of these converts are undoubtedly psychologically disturbed, although not to such an extent that they are prevented from coping with the normal stresses of society. Fundamentalist beliefs provide them with certainties that remove the need to cope with the strains of doubt and spiritual uncertainty – as they do for all who embrace fundamentalism. It would, however, be unjust to condemn all fundamentalists on this account, but there is no escaping the fact that some of them, *are* disturbed.

As an example I may cite the experience of the Reverend Kevin Tingay, Chaplain of Tone Vale Psychiatric Hospital at Taunton. Over the first three months of 1992 he had three referrals for his help: all three were Charismatic Christians of whom two had attempted suicide. On further enquiry to the nursing staff, Mr Tingay discovered that every patient of a pronounced 'religious' disposition at the hospital was either a Charismatic or an evangelical Christian. And not one patient in the hospital had any history of involvement with yoga, meditation or any other New Age activity. The sample in this instance is too small to draw any significant conclusions, but it should give those fearful authors who cite the dangers of meditation and yoga pause for thought.

Nor is the moral sense of other fundamentalists always as finely tuned as it might be. All human beings can fall from grace, and it would thus be unkind to crow over fallen televangelists and other evangelical icons of purity. But given their publicly stated high moral tone, their behaviour cannot be ignored. When the scandal of the televangelist Jim Bakker broke – it concerned his sexual abuse of a secretary, Jessica Hahn, and the misappropriation of large sums of money, for which he was later indicted for fraud and conspiracy – a fellow evangelist, the Pentecostalist John Ankerberg, sought to keep the affair out of the public eye and to deal with it in private 'according to principles set forth in scripture'. (S. Bruce, *Pray TV*, 1990, p. 203.) But Ankerberg is a man who has condemned Freemasonry, for example, as a work of darkness. When he seeks to hide wrongdoing in his own church (the Assemblies of God) he presents the image of a hypocrite.

However, hurling insults and acting in the aggressive manner of fundamentalist activists is not the way to tolerance. But neither is hiding the truth, and when the faults of would-be persecutors are germane to their activities they do merit exposure. This is especially true in the matter of 'satanic ritual abuse'. The rapid spread of this myth, and the firm hold it has taken on so many social workers, therapists and others is due in no small part to the activities of 'experts' in the field. Whether or not they deserve the label of 'expert' is another matter, but they have been influential in precipitating legal action, and thus in bringing untold misery to the innocent.

The use of so-called 'satanic indicators' as a diagnostic tool in 'satanic ritual abuse' cases followed their introduction into Britain by Pamela Klein, who has been described as 'a highly respected Chicago-based child sexual-abuse therapist'. (T. Tate, *Children for the Devil*, 1991, p.266.). The truth is rather different.

Miss Klein is not an expert on Satanism and is not professionally qualified in the field of child abuse. In February 1991, Judge Morgan Hamilton at Cook County circuit court, Illinois, ruled that she was 'not a legitimate therapist'; she is not licensed as such in the State of Illinois, while her claim to being 'a psychologist' – which resulted in her being employed by the Police Staff College at Bramshill to help develop courses on child abuse – rests on nothing more than a Bachelor's degree in psychology and sociology. (Report by Rosie Waterhouse in *The Independent on Sunday*, 24 March 1991.)

Nor is she alone among 'experts' with little qualification to underpin their expertise. Professional psychiatrists stress that specialized training is needed in all cases of child abuse, and have pointed out that 'religious faith is no substitute for professional experience and qualifications'. (Prof Hugh Freeman, Editor of the *British Journal of Psychiatry*, in *The Independent on Sunday*, 19 August 1990.) It is distressing to find a contrary view expressed by Maureen Davies.

Although she is the leader of the fundamentalist camp in the 'satanic abuse' field, Mrs Davies's views are openly hostile to secular psychiatry. She has said:

It is sad when you see the state of the Christian Church in America. To be a Christian counsellor in the Church you have to have a degree in psychotherapy, you have to be a qualified social worker. Therefore all their dealings with the problems come from a secular, humanistic, analytical point of view. They do not rely on the Holy Spirit, what God is saying or really where the person is at spiritually. And it is very obvious. ('American Trip' tape transcript, ORCRO 5, p.38)

It might be noted also that Patricia Pulling, the most prominent proponent of 'satanic abuse' in the USA claims to hold 'innumerable degrees and awards' but in fact holds no higher academic qualifications and has no clinical background to give credence to her counselling and writing.

Nor are Protestant fundamentalists the only ones to offer a specious expertise. Fr Joseph Brennan, a Roman Catholic priest of Lafayette, Louisiana, is now recognized as an 'expert' on Satanism, having been tutored by Lawrence Pazder. Fr Brennan turned to him because he is 'an expert on the subject of Satanic cults and ritualistic abuse. Because of his knowledge on these subjects, I went to British Columbia to study under him on several occasions since 1986.' (J. Brennan, *The Kingdom of Darkness*, 1989, p.21.) And so as the blind continue to lead the blind, ignorance and credulity are spread still further and the myth is perpetuated.

There are, of course, other areas in which fundamentalists and their fellow-travellers pretend to authoritative knowledge, but it is the concept of rampant, criminal Satanism that evokes the greatest degree of fear and anxiety and offers the greatest potential, through its imagined crimes, for false accusation and real suffering by the innocent. That there are depraved individuals who may utilize bizarre rituals in the course of child abuse, is both possible and probable. But satanic abuse in any meaningful sense is a chimaera – a monster created from fundamentalist fear, ignorance and prurience.

It does, however, give added scope for the activities of other fanatics who are not fundamentalist Christians. Those of them who work within the social services have a vested interest in perpetuating the myth of 'Satanism'. Once the scandalous witch-hunt at Cleveland, in which so many parents suffered from false accusations consequent upon equivocal diagnostic techniques, had given child abuse a high profile, something further was needed to maintain it. Satanism proved to be just that something; it was duly borrowed from its fundamentalist inventors and a new, self-serving industry of accusation, rescue and cure came into being; but should it be permitted to flourish? A tolerant society will necessarily admit the right of anyone to hold bizarre beliefs, but those beliefs should not be allowed to bring grief and distress to the innocent.

And it should oppose even more strenuously efforts to enshrine such folly in the criminal code. In America three States have already passed legislation against 'satanic' activity. 'Ritual Mutilation' is now a specific offence in Illinois (Amendment to Criminal Code Sec. 12–31, Ch. 38, approved 8 September 1989), but why 'wounding with intent' or 'grievous bodily harm' should be inadequate to cover this is not made clear. Similarly in Louisiana, 'ritualistic acts' involving mutilation, torture or worse, are now specifically illegal. There can be no argument against prohibiting such acts, but by separating them out from other forms of bodily harm the way is left open to prohibit any organization that may be suspected (or accused) of engaging in them. In Idaho specific legislation (House Bill 817) concerning 'ritualized child abuse' passed into law on 3 April 1990. Again, one cannot dissent from the intention, but it must be emphasized that it implies an acceptance of the reality of something for which no substantive evidence has yet been produced – anywhere.

In all these cases the vested interests of 'Christian' law officers, and the pressure groups with which they are involved, were at work. That such laws could be passed without strenuous opposition from civil liberty groups is an indication of the success of fundamentalist propaganda. Misinformation on all matters relating to 'criminal' cult and occult activity is disseminated among law enforcement agencies through the File 18 Newsletters, issued by Lt Larry Jones of the Cult Crime

Network Inc at Boise, Idaho. Justification for introducing leg-islation of this kind is specious in the extreme. There is little enough evidence that crimes of this nature, with a specific ritual element, are committed at all; and claims that ritual murders are common but that the evidence just cannot be found are simply absurd. The point was taken up by Ken Lanning of the FBI, who argued that on the basis of Uniform Crime Report statistics (some 20,000 murders per year in the USA): 'There just flat out aren't enough missing people to account for all the ritual murders that police officials such as Jones believe are occurring.'

This argument was countered by Lt Jones with some strange logic. The statistics, he argued, reflect 'only those crimes reported to police, not the unreported ones!' He continues:

> Some (perhaps many) traditionally-committed murders go unreported for five, ten, twenty years and even forever. *These* are not tabulated into UCR totals because they are not reduced to writing on a local police officer's report form . . . [Further] Ample information now exists which logically describes how and why satanic serial killers can perpetually escape exposure, police scrutiny and prosecution. (File 18 Newsletter, No 4, October 1989)

He does not make clear, however, just what this information is.

Which is, of course, the weakness in his armour and in that of those who argue in the same manner. If this nonsensical approach to crime – effectively that the absence of any evidence of a crime is a form of proof that it took place – is publicized, then the public at large will begin to perceive how foolish are the persistent cries of 'Wolf!' from the fundamentalist camp.

They will also, perhaps, begin to perceive the danger of campaigns for legal restrictions on activities that can be described as 'occult'. Geoffrey Dickens has long sought to persuade Parliament to legislate against the occult (*see* p.55 above), as has Richard Cottrell whose attempt to restrict the lawful activities of the New Religious Movements was defeated because sufficient alarm was raised among both Christian and non-Christian religious bodies to enable effective protests against the proposal to be mounted. The danger with attempts to restrict beliefs or practices that can be labelled 'occult' – however inappropriate the label may be – is that the negative image generated by hostile fundamentalist propaganda is already deeply entrenched in the popular mind, and sympathy would thus be difficult to gain.

The only effective response is to ensure that the public is well and accurately informed on such topics, and this will require challenging every newspaper, radio and television report or interview that gives biased or distorted accounts or that presents fiction as fact. Television programmes are especially dangerous in this respect; radio cannot present a visual image, and replies and critical comments in newspapers are forgotten all too soon – newspapers, it must be remembered, are among the most ephemeral of printed documents. Against this the television documentary can be preserved on videotape and presented again and again; it can also be repackaged and distributed as a commercial, sectarian video.[2] However false the image is, the power of pictorial imagery is enormous, and it is reinforced at every showing.

So far anti-cult and anti-occult fundamentalist propaganda of this nature is still rather a blunt-edged weapon; it has not yet been distributed to children – who are necessarily more vulnerable to it – nor would it be permitted in state schools. But there is a growing movement to found specifically 'Christian' schools – by which is meant not the traditional Church of England school, but an institution funded by and presenting the viewpoint of specifically evangelical and Charismatic Christian groups. This they have a legal right to do, but if the movement grows significantly, then a substantial number of children will be removed from the pluralist arena and will become less receptive to the ideal of tolerance.

Nor is this problem confined only to 'Christian' schools. There is increasing intolerance in the Muslim community which has led, for example, to a Birmingham school removing pictures and plastic models of pigs in order not to offend the sensitivities of Muslim children and their parents. The pig has also been 'excluded as a teaching tool' at Montgomery Primary School, leading to an anti-Muslim reaction that has brought death threats to the headmaster for taking note of Muslim wishes. He is clearly placed in an impossible position in such a situation – whatever he does it will cause offence. (*The Independent on Sunday*, 10 November 1991.)

Jews face a similar dilemma. The highly provocative missionary movement 'Jews for Jesus' is to open an office in London, and there is understandable anxiety amongst orthodox Jews that they have been 'targeted' for conversion. Their fears have been articulated in an article by the Reverend Martin Kettle on the Jewish community in his parish at Barnet in North London:

> What they are alarmed about is the possibility of manipulative and underhand conversionism: the exploiting by fundamentalist Christians of the immaturity of the young and of the vulnerability of the emotionally deprived or traumatized. ('Jews need to know where they stand', in *Church Times*, 20 March 1992)

But can a truly tolerant society deny the rights of the believer to evangelize? The difficulties of such situations are brought sharply into focus when this question is faced. Commenting on this issue, Clive Calver, General Director of the Evangelical Alliance, stated that, 'to suggest that our Jewish neighbours should be denied the right to hear the Christian message is surely a form of anti-Semitism, because it excludes Jewish people specifically on grounds of race and religion'. (*Church Times*, 27 March 1992.)

The answer lies in permitting believers of all religions to put their case to those of other faiths, provided that it is done peacefully and courteously without any attempt at coercive conversion. This, however, is a counsel of perfection. And how many of those who would concur with such a sentiment would be happy to permit proselytizing by Hindus, by 'Moonies' or by witches? To be consistent in their tolerance they would have to accept it, but the negative images built up by fundamentalist propaganda are now buried too deeply in the Western psyche for perfect harmony to prevail without a herculean effort to achieve it by those who can stand back from the urge to persecute.

Even so, it can be achieved. But it will be in the face of powerful efforts to impose a narrow and limiting form of Christianity upon most of the populace, which may become increasingly receptive to them. In America there is an apparent collapse of the social consensus that has, for many years, upheld a basically compassionate society founded largely on the principles of liberal Protestantism. In its place there seem to be only the stark alternatives of chaos or the authoritarianism

– in religion as well as in social life – of one of the many forms of the amorphous New Christian Right; and fear will lead to the certain rejection of chaos.

This scenario is not a certain vision of the future, but it is a possibility that hovers on the brink of probability. If it becomes a reality, then it will give an enormous boost to the forces of religious reaction in this country also, and maintaining a legally guaranteed tolerance for minority faiths will become increasingly difficult. There is also the danger that the political authoritarianism that would inevitably accompany it would be an unknown quantity, rendering it impossible to predict just who would become the object of persecution.

We are, as yet, far away from such a situation, but it is an ever-present possibility. To combat it we must make a stand against all religious oppression; we must ensure that error and deceit are opposed by fact and by the truth; and we must work to ensure that future generations learn objective truth about the beliefs and practices of alternative faiths. If this can be achieved it will do more than guarantee religious freedom; it will also undermine attempts by self-serving politicians to manipulate the forces of fundamentalism for their own ends; and it will prevent the drawing down of blinds on the borders of orthodox science.

But it will require more than intellectual assent. Each one of us must take an active part in the struggle to preserve our liberties of mind and spirit, and in that struggle we must not forget, as the nominally Christian enemies of tolerance choose to do, that Christ did not command his followers only to love God; he also said, 'you shall love your neighbour as yourself.' Unless we act in that spirit we shall not attain our goal.

NOTES TO CHAPTER NINE

1. He is wrong about the Knights Templar; the Cathars; the Kabbalah; seventeenth century witchcraft trials; Dr Dee; the Golden Dawn; Crowley; Hitler; Dennis Wheatley; and much else besides.
2. A recent example is *Devil Worship: the Rise of Satanism*, made in 1989 by Jeremiah Films, and distributed by the Reachout Trust. It cannot be called an objective documentary by any standard.

Appendices

APPENDIX 1

Reachout Trust, which is based in Surrey in the UK, is a registered charity and a member of the Evangelical Alliance. The Trust defines itself as 'a Christian Ministry to those in the cults and occult' and its published aims are:

- To examine the beliefs of various cult and occult groups in order to present the Christian Gospel to people involved in them.

- To teach Christians, through literature, seminars, etc. a relevant way to share with such people the reality of a personal relationship with Jesus Christ.

- To co-operate with other organizations, working in the same field, in order that we can provide a complete service of counselling and help to all enquirers; whether they be Christians, those involved in the cults or occult or family members of those involved.

APPENDIX 2

Extracts from a Cultists Anonymous pamphlet were reproduced in *The Quarterly Review* of the Churches' Fellowship for Psychical and Spiritual Studies, Number 136, Summer 1988. Included in the list of the marks of cults were the following examples:

- Meaningful communication with family and former friends is sharply curtailed and the cult becomes the convert's new

Family. In most cults every attempt is made to blur or eliminate the convert's conscious memories of their former way of life and personal history.

• Converts may display symptoms of extreme tension and stress, fear, guilt, lack of humour, regression in communication skills/critical judgement/judgement-logic skills and reality-testing.

Among the possible effects on a convert of remaining in a cult for even a short period were said to be:

• Impaired capacity to form judgements and to think.

• The convert's potential for adjusting back to normal living after leaving the cult deteriorates according to the length of cult involvement. There comes a point of no return, depending on the cult and the individual, after which the person is beyond rescue.

The points readers were warned to remember included the following:

• Deceptive techniques may be used to recruit members and solicit donations. The identity of the cult is often deliberately hidden.

• Never, under any circumstances, give money to a group of individuals unless you are totally convinced of their legitimacy. Money collected for 'the poor' or for 'youth ministry projects' may go to a destructive cult instead.

Under the heading 'Beware of Recruiters', it was stated that very few people set out to become members of cults, and that unless they met a recruiter there was little likelihood of anyone joining a cult, however vulnerable they might be. People were also advised to:

Beware of people with simplistic answers or solutions to complex world problems.
There are no easy answers.

Beware of people who recruit you through guilt.
Guilt induced by others is rarely a productive emotion.

APPENDIX 3

The list of areas that could open the door to the occult, given in Roy Livesey's *More Understanding the New Age*, included the following in a list of 145 subjects under the heading 'Occult':

Hatha Yoga
Handwriting Analysis
Horoscopes
Hypnosis
'Dungeons and Dragons'
Taoism
T'ai Chi Chuan
Karate
Mascots
Fantasy role-playing games
Martial Arts
Judo
Parapsychology
Psychoanalysis
Freud
Buddhas
Indian elephants
Myths

He listed 80 cults to beware of including:

Lourdes
Madonna and Child
Marxism
Moral Rearmament
Roman Catholicism
Modernism, liberalism and the social gospel
Saints
Communism
Islam (Mohammedism) [sic]
Hinduism
Buddhism
Pagan tourist places
Belief systems
Transcendental Meditation

The following were included in a list of 120 'Holistic Healing Therapies' which again could 'open the door to the occult':

Acupuncture
Osteopathy
Contemplative Prayer
The Placebo
Holistic Cosmetics

Homoeopathy
Interpersonal Relationships
Positive Thinking

APPENDIX 4

The File 18 Newsletters are compiled and published by the Cult
Crime Impact Network Inc., of Boise, Idaho, in the United States.
They carry a disclaimer to the effect that they are for use in the
detection of criminal activity and the protection of citizens, and not
meant to interfere with First Amendment rights.

The December 1988 Newsletter explains that it is a bi-monthly
newsletter written primarily for law enforcement and members
of the criminal justice system, the purpose of which is to inform
and educate on matters dealing with the occult, occult-motivated
crimes and deviant movement groups. It is written with the aid
of police contributors and others who have encountered destructive, non-traditional group activities or are investigating bizarre
and unconventional crimes with occult overtones. The compilees
believe that sharing factual information about real crimes, available
resources, gathered intelligence, and announcements of upcoming
seminars and in-service training will raise police awareness and
encourage local networking of cult/occult *crime* information. More
than 1,500 subscribers from across the United States now receive
regular intelligence and training information about cult and occult
groups and events through the File 18 Newsletter.

   File 18 is written *by* law enforcement professionals *for* law
enforcement; and yet, C.C.I.N. is not directly affiliated with or
funded by any police agency. Printing, mailing, and administrative
expenses are totally underwritten by contributions from the readers
and others interested in combating occult crime. C.C.I.N. is a tax
exempt, non-profit corporation.

Bibliography

This bibliography is necessarily selective and does not include every book referred to in the text, but it does list all those titles that are of particular importance. Many of them contain bibliographies or guides to further reading. It should also be noted that comments on the titles listed represent my personal opinions and are not necessarily indicative of general critical reception of the books in question.

Anderson, Peter, *Satan's Snare: The Influence of the Occult*, Evangelical Press, 1988.
Far from providing 'invaluable information', as the cover claims, it reflects the opinions of its author, 'an evangelist with Christian Ministries'.

Ankerberg, John and Weldon, John, *The Secret Teachings of the Masonic Lodge, A Christian Perspective*, Moody Press, 1990.
A detailed analysis of the structure of Freemasonry and of American masonic rituals (which differ from those in use in Britain). It is a subtle attack using specious arguments and much false information.

Barker, Eileen, *New Religious Movements, a practical introduction*, HMSO, 1989.
A valuable survey of the major cults that deals also with the problems of de-programming and the relations between converts and their families. The author adopts a neutral, academic approach.

Bambridge, A.D., *Acupuncture Investigated*, Diasozo Trust, 1989.
——, *Homoeopathy Investigated*, Diasozo Trust.
Neither work (the second title is a 36 page pamphlet) is a true 'investigation', offering instead a biased vision of these two 'alternative therapies'.

Boa, Kenneth, *Cults, World Religions, and You*, Victor Books, 1977.
A widely used guide for group study but it does not live up to its claim to be 'thorough' and 'simply explained'; it is inaccurate over many factual details.

Bobgan, Martin and Deirdre, *Hypnosis and the Christian*, Bethany House, 1984.
A hostile 'appraisal' of the subject setting out the fundamentalist view of hypnosis.

Boyd, Andrew, *Blasphemous Rumours. Is Satanic Ritual Abuse Fact or Fantasy? An Investigation*, Fount, 1991.
The author finds in favour of fact and gives a number of case histories, but his arguments do not stand up to objective analysis.

Brennan, Joseph, *The Kingdom of Darkness*, Acadian House, 1989.
A popular work on Satanism, of value only in showing that credulity is not confined to Protestant fundamentalists.

Bruce, Steve, *The Rise and Fall of the New Christian Right. Conservative Protestant Politics in America 1978–1988*, Clarendon Press, 1988.
——, *Pray TV. Televangelism in American*, Routledge, 1990.
Both works are models of rigorous, academic analysis and of great value in understanding the structure and nature of institutionalized intolerance.

Campbell, Eileen, and Brennan, J.H., *The Aquarian Guide to the New Age*, Aquarian Press, 1990.
The New Age's view of itself, but as full of errors as are hostile studies of the subject.

Cole, Michael, Graham, Jim, Higton, Tony and Lewis, David, *What is the New Age?*, Hodder & Stoughton, 1990.
An evangelical vision of the New Age – as lacking in objectivity and as prone to error as Campbell and Brennan's 'Guide'.

Crim, Keith (ed.), *Abingdon Dictionary of Living Religions*, Abingdon, 1981.
A sound, scholarly reference work with accurate and concise accounts of major and minor religions, sects and cults.

Cumbey, Constance E., *The Hidden Dangers of the Rainbow. The New Age Movement and Our Coming Age of Barbarism*, Huntington House, 1983.
An unreliable attack on the New Age, yet typical of fundamentalist polemic.

Enroth, Ronald, *Youth, Brainwashing, and the Extremist Cults*, Paternoster Press, 1977.
A survey of the major cults, and relatively objective given its hostile viewpoint.

Ferguson, Marilyn, *The Aquarian Conspiracy. Personal and Social Transformation in the 1980s*, Routledge, 1981.
The classical apologia for the New Age and a prime target for fundamentalist attacks.

Gardner, Richard A., *Sex Abuse Hysteria. Salem Witch Trials Revisited*, Creative Therapeutics, 1991.

A scholarly study which is a necessary corrective to the wealth of credulous nonsense written on sex abuse in general and ritual abuse in particular.

Gordon, Ian, *The Craft and the Cross*, Kingsway, 1989.
A hostile study of Freemasonry by a 'freed Mason' who is now a charismatic Christian.

Hamill, John, *The Craft. A History of English Freemasonry*, Crucible, 1986.
A dispassionate study that acts as a corrective to the unbalanced accounts of anti-Masons.

Harper, Audrey, *Dance with the Devil*, Kingsway, 1990.
Although presented as a 'true' story, this more in the nature of fantasy.

Hart, Lowell, *Satan's Music Exposed*, Photo Commentary by Salem Kirban, Kirban, 1980.
The classic evangelical attack upon Rock music, and especially its use in Christian worship.

Irvine, Doreen, *From Witchcraft to Christ*, Concordia, 1973.
The sensational, popular, and highly implausible account of a conversion to Christianity by a supposed witch.

Johnston, Jerry, *The Edge of Evil. The Rise of Satanism in North America*, Foreword by Geraldo Rivera, Word, 1989.
An influential but uncritical and flawed study by a popular 'expert' on youth culture. The author's high media profile has ensured that his one-sided views are highly publicised.

Lawrence, John, *Freemasonry – a religion?*, Kingsway, 1987.
A popular argument, by an Anglican minister, for the incompatibility of Freemasonry with Christianity.

LeBar, James J., *Cults, Sects, and the New Age*, Our Sunday Visitor, 1989.
A relatively objective study, but necessarily with a negative bias, from a Roman Catholic viewpoint.

Livesey, Roy, *Understanding the New Age, World Government and World Religion*, New Wine, 1989.
——, *More Understanding the New Age. Discerning Anti-Christ and the Occult Revival*, New Wine, 1990.
——, *Understanding Deception. New Age Teaching in the Church*, New Wine, 1987.
A trilogy of denunciations of every aspect of the New Age. (Two other books by the same author concern his own 'escape' from New Age bondage, and alternative medicine.)

Logan, Kevin, *Paganism and the Occult, A Manifesto for Christian Action*, Kingsway, 1988.
The author's aim is to provide the basis for converting occultists to Christianity, but his lack of objectivity and of factual accuracy remove credibility from his attempt.

Martin, Walter, *The Kingdom of the Cults*, Bethany House, 1985.
The standard study of cults and non-orthodox Christian denominations from the evangelical viewpoint.
——, *The New Age Cult*, Bethany House, 1989.
A 'militant refutation' of the New Age that is much less reasoned than the author's major work.

Morran, Elda Susan, and Schlemmer, Lawrence, *Faith for the Fearful? An investigation into new churches in the greater Durban area*, Centre for Applied Social Sciences, University of Natal, 1984.
An important sociological survey (commissioned by the established churches of Durban) the conclusions of which are valid for Europe and North America as well as for urban South Africa.

Parker, Russ, *The Occult. Deliverance from Evil*, Inter-Varsity Press, 1989.
An uncritical and heavily biased study by an Anglican minister.

Perry, Michael (ed.), *Deliverance. Psychic Disturbances and Occult Involvement*, SPCK, 1987.
Primarily a pastoral handbook by The Christian Exorcism Study Group. While much of the book is not relevant to questions of intolerance, the chapters on occultism are: they are also the only wholly unreliable sections of the text.

Pulling, Pat, *The Devil's Web. Who is Stalking Your Children for Satan?*, Huntington House, 1989.
A sensational attack on occult involvement, drawing in child abuse, rock music and fantasy role-playing games. It suffers from a lack of both objectivity and factual accuracy.

Raschke, Carl A., *Painted Black. From Drug Killings to Heavy Metal – the alarming true story of how Satanism is terrorizing our Communities*, Harper & Row, 1990.
The combination of a respected academic author and a major publisher should ensure objectivity and reliability, but it does neither and the book's sensational nature does nothing for the cause of tolerance.

Ross, Joan Carol, and Langone, Michael D., *Cults. What parents should know. A practical guide to help parents with children in destructive groups*, Lyle Stuart, 1988.
Although ostensibly reasonable and tolerant in tone, the underlying hostility to cults in general (the book is published for the American Family Foundation) does not help to promote any sense of real tolerance of alternative beliefs.

Short, Martin, *Inside the Brotherhood. Further Secrets of the Freemasons*, Grafton, 1989.
A sequel to *The Brotherhood*, Stephen Knight's attack on Freemasonry. It is overly hostile and factually unreliable.

Smith, Michelle and Pazder, Lawrence, *Michelle Remembers*, Michael Joseph, 1981.

The fantastic 'true story' that helped to launch the whole unhappy saga of so-called 'Satanic Ritual Abuse'.

Tate, Tim, *Children for the Devil. Ritual abuse and satanic crime*, Methuen, 1991.
Because of the controversial nature of the subject the author makes much of his secular stance, but he maintains all the credulity of the fundamentalist and argues for the reality of 'satanic crime'.

The following periodicals are also extremely useful for further information:

Quarterly Journal of the Churches Fellowship for Psychical and Spiritual Studies (in progress).
Each issue contains a survey of media reports and comments relating to the supernatural, the occult and the New Age.

Orco, The Occult Response to the Christian Response to the Occult Magazine, edited by Peter Elliott, 1989–1990.
Seven issues appeared before publication ceased. They are invaluable for verbatim reprints and transcripts of lectures, articles and audio-tapes by the more vitriolic opponents of occultism and the New Age (eg Maureen Davies, Dianne Core, John Todd and Larry Jones), together with responses – variously reasoned and equally vitriolic – to them.

Index

Note: Specific world religions and major denominations within Christianity are not included in this index.